CULTS
What Parents Should Know

D1507805

CULTS
What Parents Should Know

A practical guide to help parents
with children in destructive groups

William C. Reynolds

A LYLE STUART BOOK
Published by Carol Publishing Group

Copyright © 1988 by the American Family Foundation. A Lyle Stuart Book. Published by Carol Publishing Group. Editorial Offices 600 Madison Avenue, New York, NY 10022. Sales & Distribution Offices 120 Enterprise Avenue, Secaucus, NJ 07094. In Canada: Musson Book Company, a division of General Publishing Co. Limited, Don Mills, Ontario. All rights reserved. No part of this book may be reproduced in any form, except by a newspaper or magazine reviewer who wishes to quote brief passages in connection with a review. Queries regarding rights and permissions should be addressed to: Carol Publishing Group. 600 Madison Avenue, New York, NY 10022. Manufactured in the U.S.A.

Library of Congress Cataloging-in-Publication-Data

Ross, Joan Carol, 1951–
    Cults : what parents should know.

    1. Cults. 2. Parent and child. I. Langone,
Michael D. II. Title.
BP603.R67 1988   291   88-71489
ISBN 0-8184-0511-2

About the Authors

Joan Carol Ross, Ed. M., formerly on the staff of the American Family Foundation (the publisher of this book) has been a writer, educator, and family counselor in the field of cult awareness for nearly ten years. Ms. Ross, who is married and the mother of a young son, Benjamin, was a member of the Divine Light Mission for six years before being deprogrammed by Ted Patrick. She earned her Ed. M. in Counseling from Harvard Graduate School of Education in 1981.

Michael D. Langone, Ph.D., Director of Research and Education for the American Family Foundation, is a licensed psychologist who has worked with more than 125 former cult members and their families. Editor of the scholarly *Cultic Studies Journal,* Dr. Langone has studied cults for the past decade while publishing and lecturing extensively on the subject.

The American Family Foundation (AFF)

is a non-profit, tax-exempt, research and educational organization founded in 1979. Staffed by professionals and guided by a distinguished advisory board, AFF collects information on cults and manipulative techniques of persuasion and control, analyzes the information in order to advance understanding of the problem and possible solutions to it, and shares this understanding with professionals, the general public, and those needing help with cult involvements.

AFF • Box 336 • Weston, Massachusetts 02193 • (617) 893-0930

Contents

Introduction

During the past fifteen years, thousands of media reports, articles, expert testimonies in legal cases, and legislative hearings have described harmful activities associated with political, psychological, and religious cults.

Although estimates vary, there are probably at least a thousand cults in the United States and Europe. Many of these groups are harmless, but many others have incalculably damaged hundreds of thousands of families and individuals. Most of these groups are relatively small, but some have tens of thousands of members and incomes of many millions of dollars a year. It seems probable that more than one million Americans have been members of cults during the last twenty years.

During the late 1960s and early 1970s, when a major expansion in cult recruitment of middle-class youth began, few people understood cults or the problems associated with them, and virtually no resources were available for affected families and individuals. In those days, the parents of many cult recruits were frightened by sudden and profound personality changes observed in their children. Few friends, neighbors, or professionals appreciated the plight of these parents. As such parents began to communicate with one another, however, some came to realize that children from other families demonstrated similarly frightening changes in language, demeanor, and behavior. Many of the young people who were caught up in cults seemed cast from the same mold, "programmed" like robots.* Not knowing where to turn or what to do, some parents took matters into their own hands. They seized their children, forced them to stay at home or in a motel room, and tried to "talk sense into them." The term "deprogramming" was adopted to describe the awakening of the cultist's mind during this process.

It soon became apparent that the key element in liberating cult members from a group's hold was helping them reconnect with family members and hear facts and ideas from which they had been isolated. In addition, as deprogrammed former cultists began to assist in the deprogramming of others, an underground network of deprogrammers developed. A growing number of parents turned to them for help.

---

* The terms "mind control," "brainwashing," "coercive persuasion," and "thought reform" have all been used to describe the processes through which cults gain unusually powerful influence over individuals.

Involuntary deprogramming was an ethically problematical, sometimes legally risky (failed deprogrammings not infrequently resulted in suits against deprogrammers and parents — and occasionally in jail terms), and very expensive procedure ($10,000 being a low fee for travel, security, lodging, and consultants). However appealing this procedure seemed to some distressed parents, it was not a viable option for the majority. In recent years, however, mental health professionals with an interest in this area have helped parents devise reasonably effective and ethical strategies for assisting cult-involved children voluntarily to reevaluate their cult affiliations and return to normal life.* As more information about such options has become available, parents have turned more frequently to them.

Despite increased understanding about methods of helping cultists voluntarily reevaluate their cult affiliation, few published guidelines exist, and those that do exist do not analyze the problem in sufficient detail. In order to remedy this deficiency, we and our colleagues at the American Family Foundation decided to write and publish this book, a practical manual designed to help parents whose child may be involved in a cult.

This book is not a "cookbook." As we make clear again and again, *every case is unique. Cults: What Parents Should Know,* however, can give parents a structure for understanding their particular problem, can direct their questioning and search for information, and can provide some practical suggestions.

We intentionally avoid listing "bad groups" in order to emphasize the parents' responsibility to find out about the cult to which *their* child belongs. In the final analysis, the parents' concern, sensitivity, perseverance, and intelligence are their most important assets.

This book began with a series of discussions between the authors and two colleagues at the American Family Foundation, Rev. Roger Daly and Dr. John G. Clark. Dr. Clark, an Assistant Clinical Professor of Psychiatry at Harvard Medical School, is a pioneer in this field, having worked with over 1,000 parents and cultists. Combined, the four of us have worked with nearly 1,500 persons.

---

* One group of professionals, reporting on nineteen cult-related mental health consultations, achieved positive outcomes in approximately two-thirds of their cases (Steve K. Dubrow Eichel et al., "Mental Health Related Interventions in Cult-related Cases: Preliminary Investigation of Outcomes," *Cultic Studies Journal,* Vol. 1, No., 2, Fall/Winter 1984, pages 156-166.) These results compare favorably to success rates for involuntary deprogramming, which appears to result in the cultist leaving the cult approximately two-thirds of the time (M. Langone, "Deprogramming: An Analysis of Parental Questionnaires," *Cultic Studies Journal,* Vol. 1, No. 1, Spring/Summer 1984, pages 63-78).

The authors, then, owe a special debt of gratitude to Dr. Clark and Rev. Daly. Their experience helps anchor this book in the real-life problems of real people.

We also wish to acknowledge Linda Blood, Robert E. Schecter, David Todd, and Eleanor Clark. Their technical assistance in the preparation of this manuscript has been vital.

Also contributing to the publication of this book were members of the Boston affiliate of the Cult Awareness Network, in particular: Bob and Mary Crockett; George and Virginia McCarthy; LeeAnne, Nancy, and Phil Pellegrini; Ann Smith; and Carol Turnbull.

A special debt of gratitude is owed the Trustees of the Nathaniel and Elizabeth P. Stevens Foundation, whose financial support made the printing of this book possible.

Joan Carol Ross, Ed. M.
Michael D. Langone, Ph. D.
May 1988

Chapter One

A Case Study*

Mona Wood was attractive, friendly, and outgoing as a teenager — a class officer in high school. Endowed with curiosity and a scientific mind, she set about exploring some of the deeper human questions. She wanted to know what, precisely, was the purpose of life. She questioned the usefulness of religion. She wondered what her own role should be as a responsible adult.

For all of these questions, Mona sought clear, rational answers. She was especially excited about college, which she envisioned as a place to do some rigorous thinking, satisfy her intellectual curiosity, and broaden her social sphere.

In the fall of 1970 Mona arrived at college, high-spirited and expectant. She had enjoyed the long drive out there with her parents, and in some ways she was glad that the college she had chosen was many miles away from home. She was ready for a new beginning, and the distance made it seem more real.

Mr. and Mrs. Wood helped Mona unload her belongings and then headed home. Finally alone, Mona surveyed her new room tentatively — the brown cardboard boxes, neatly labelled, stuffed to the brim with her personal belongings, the built-in dormitory desk that was just like everyone else's, the narrow bed, and the bare, mint-green walls. Taking a deep breath, Mona realized that her initial excitement had dissipated, and that she felt very disoriented and lost, adrift in these new surroundings, hundreds of miles from all that was familiar. For a moment, Mona was overcome by a loneliness deeper than any she had experienced before.

By the following week, classes had begun and the campus was bustling with activity. Mona had always been a diligent student, and she was somewhat disappointed in her classmates, who seemed more interested in having a good time than in serious learning. They apparently had come from very wealthy, socially-sophisticated families, and Mona felt different, out of place, an oddity. She wrote her parents, "I'm the only one here who hasn't been to Europe several times."

---

* This case has been chosen as an illustration because a) the parents and ex-cultist were available, articulate, and extremely cooperative, and b) their experiences are very similar to those of other persons adversely affected by cults.

After receiving a number of troubling letters from Mona, Mr. and Mrs. Wood became apprehensive about their daughter's emotional well-being. They asked themselves, "Did we protect her too much? Is she really happy? Or, are we wishing she were unhappy because we miss her and want her to come home? Not wanting to overreact, the Woods consoled themselves by reasoning that Mona was probably fine, and that she could benefit from these new, albeit uncomfortable, experiences. They diagnosed their own anxiety as "empty nest syndrome." Mona was, after all, their last child to leave home.

First semester, Mona took a religion course that reawakened many of her own religious doubts. At the same time, she stopped going to church. It just wasn't satisfying her spiritual needs. It didn't provide adequate answers. There were too many incongruities, she thought. Too much hypocrisy.

Mona voiced her religious concerns to her parents, who encouraged her to "try and have faith." But Mona couldn't buy it. She had no tolerance for ambiguity. She wanted definite answers, not faith.

Mona's growing aversion towards her religion made the Woods uneasy. They couldn't pinpoint why, but they had a gut feeling that something more than religion was disturbing their daughter.

The Woods visited during parents' weekend, which came six weeks into the semester. During their visit, Mona confessed that she felt very insecure about her academic and social capabilities. Wanting to help, the Woods went to the school counselor and asked, "Should Mona stay here? Is she capable?" They were told, "She's a very capable girl. She's just going through an adjustment period."

In the fall of 1971, when she entered her sophomore year, Mona seemed to withdraw abruptly from almost all extra-curricular activities. She stopped ice skating — one of her loves since childhood — and lost interest in photography. She also started spending a good deal of time studying the Bible and attending a Bible fellowship group.

The Woods were concerned. Not only did Mona seem to be cutting herself off socially, but her academic work appeared to be suffering as well. Within two semesters, she had changed her major several times. She had started as a chemistry major and by her second year she was majoring in fine arts. Her father pressed her, "What are you going to do with a fine arts degree?" Mona seemed unusually defensive and unable to justify her decisions, which left the Woods even more perplexed. Again they asked themselves, "Is something wrong? With her? With us?" And they made arrangements to visit Mona, hoping to get a better understanding of what was happening to their daughter.

Cults: What Parents Should Know

Upon their arrival, the Woods noticed a dramatic change in Mona's demeanor. She seemed unusually subdued, distant, secretive. When she did talk, it was clumsy and unspontaneous, except — and the Woods thought this rather peculiar — when she was talking about her new interest in the Bible and when she was with the fellowship group. On these occasions Mona came alive. She seemed more herself — animated, confident, and secure.

At Mona's request the Woods attended a fellowship meeting. It appeared to be an innocuous discussion about the Bible and Christianity. Conversing with some of the members, they inquired whether the group interfered with one's religion and were told, "no." After the meeting the Woods asked Mona more about the fellowship, "but not in great detail because she tended to clam up. She'd say, 'I don't want to talk about it,' go into her dorm room, and slam the door. She reacted to our questions as though we were subjecting her to some type of criminal interrogation."

Disquieted by their visit, the Woods wondered why they were having so much trouble communicating with their daughter. Perhaps they weren't phrasing their questions carefully enough. Admittedly, Mr. Wood may have aggravated the situation by his demand for concise yes or no answers. And yes, he had raised his voice uncharacteristically, losing his temper more than once over Mona's defensiveness and apparent unwillingness (or was it inability?) to participate in rational discussion.

But was it all their fault? Mona seemed so unreachable. So distant. She responded to questions by quoting scripture or parroting phrases she had heard at the fellowship meetings. The Woods speculated that Mona might be using the group as a crutch to support her through a turbulent time. Maybe everything would work out.

Late in her sophomore year, Mona made a formal commitment to join the fellowship. Despite some minor concerns — was the group really Christian? was it taking Mona out of the mainstream of college life? — the Woods conceded that it was probably a good choice.

They recalled, "When Mona was in high school she was approached by Scientology. She wanted $300 to take one of their courses. We had a tremendous argument and, when we didn't give her the money, she didn't pursue it any further. A few years later she started going to a meditation group, but quit that when she left for college. So when she wanted to join a Bible fellowship we said, 'Thank God she's interested in something normal, something we can relate to. That sounds great!' We really thought she was joining a wonderful group of young people interested in the Bible, with whom she felt comfortable. And the school recognized them, even gave them a house to live in. We spoke to college personnel and to our own priest, and everybody told us that the group was okay, that Mona was just going through a phase, and that we had nothing to worry about. Besides, other parents with children in the group did not seem concerned."

As time went on, however, the Woods became increasingly uneasy with Mona's behavior. On visits home, for instance, Mona's attempts to be sociable would last for about 24 hours, after which she would almost predictably retreat to her room, isolating herself from both family and friends while making plans to attend a cult "fellowship." It was obvious to everyone who had known her before college that she had undergone some disturbing change in personality. She couldn't concentrate. She couldn't communicate. She couldn't even make simple decisions.

In the summer of 1972 Mona came home and got a job working with children at a local playground. She had done this type of work before and had enjoyed it immensely, but this time she was very uncomfortable and unsure of herself. On several occasions she dissolved into tears over her inability to handle the children. At this point even Mona felt that something was wrong, and she went to a counseling center to seek help.

The Woods also went to the center, at Mona's request. They were advised there that Mona was depressed, and that she was very immature, and that they should take her out of school and make her go to work, get therapy, and resolve her "developmental conflicts." Looking for a second opinion, the Woods went to a psychiatric social worker who told them "not to take her out of school but instead to insist that Mona finish her four years, lest she quit and never go back."

Confronted with these various professional opinions, the Woods decided to analyze the situation themselves. They thought about Mona's upbringing, and the role each of them had played in it. They were desperate to understand what was happening to their daughter, why she had become to terribly withdrawn, insecure, and incompetent. After a great deal of self-searching, arguing and discussing, they concluded that Mona's immaturity was at least in part due to "our overprotectiveness." She always knew that if a problem arose she could pick up the telephone and call us. As a result, she never really learned to solve her own problems. Instead, she passed them on to us. And we would try to solve them for her. We never quite stepped out of the caretaker role."

The Woods also felt that Mona's development had been hampered by an upbringing that "encouraged her to develop a naive idealism, a belief that all people are basically good. So she ended up accepting people at face value: those who looked good were good; those who looked bad obviously were bad. But she didn't know how to evaluate people on a deeper level. For that, she relied on us."

Disturbed by their own role in hindering Mona's development, the Woods tried to engage their daughter in more adult ways — encouraging her to make choices, to take responsibility for her actions. When she called with a problem, the Woods would urge her to try and solve it herself. But Mona balked at this responsibility, and leaned more and more heavily upon the Bible fellowship for emotional support and for a sense of identity and purpose.

In 1973, Mona graduated from college, but with poor grades, and became more deeply involved in the fellowship. She took a job as an aide at a rehabilitation center — planning to study occupational therapy in graduate school — and moved into an apartment with three other girls where they hosted group meetings and based their intense recruiting effort. Mona was now preoccupied with becoming a fellowship leader. After a year, however, Mona's little apartment-based group disbanded and she returned home.

She was very depressed, and went for counseling to a psychiatric social worker. Unfortunately, he knew little about cults and did not really understand what she was telling him about her experience. The social worker told Mona's parents that she was too idealistic and could not face the "real world." Conflict with her parents increased, and Mona left home again, this time to spend a year in a nearby state assisting in a fellowship member's unsuccessful run for Congress. After a few months on the campaign trail, however, Mona was persuaded by two male members of the group — following an all-night discussion with her — to enroll at the fellowship's college to be trained as a "Leader." She asked her parents for financial help, but her father said that she would have to earn the first $1,000 for tuition herself. When she managed to do this, her father felt obliged to keep his word, and gave her the balance, much as he and his wife were against the move.

After Mona's departure for the college, her parents saw very little of her. Although she kept in touch by letter, these showed that she had changed even more. She wrote almost exclusively of her "love for Jesus" and about her total commitment to the group, seemingly unable to objectively evaluate her situation.

It wasn't until November, 1980, still very perturbed by Mona's emotional distance and inability to settle down, that the Woods felt compelled to investigate the Bible fellowship more thoroughly. Mrs. Wood had just read a series of newspaper articles describing the deaths of over 900 members of Jim Jones's People's Temple in Jonestown, Guyana. And there were additional articles describing groups which were thought to be similar to the People's Temple. These groups, labeled "destructive cults," reportedly used techniques of "mind control" to recruit and maintain their members. Mrs. Wood was both startled and frightened when she discovered Mona's fellowship group listed among others as a cult, and she passed this information on to her husband, urging him to "read this. It's important!"

After reading the articles, the Woods formed different opinions. Mr. Wood thought that the issue of cults and mind control simply did not apply to what Mona was doing. Mrs. Wood was more suspicious about the fellowship, but even she felt that, "This is ridiculous. Mona has better judgment than to get involved in something like this."

Shortly thereafter the Woods received a telephone call from a friend whose son was in a cult. She advised that Mona, too, was caught in a cult and was a victim of mind control. Mrs. Wood recalled, "She gave us a lot of material, which it took us a long time to grasp. Even then, my husband and I felt differently. He was much less inclined to believe our daughter was being subjected to mind control. But after this call, we started digging, investigating, trying to find out the real nature of the fellowship group."

The more they read about the fellowship, the more they realized it did not follow traditional Christian teachings. In fact, the version of the Bible used by the group was completely different from any they had seen, and had seemingly been translated and reinterpreted by the fellowship leader for his own self-aggrandizement. His teachings, apparently, were to be revered as the word of God.

More alarming still, the fellowship philosophy advocated that members become complacent, obedient, dedicated followers, representatives of the party line, skilled in recruitment and fund-raising for the group. According to the articles written by ex-members, deception was tolerated, even encouraged, if it were necessary to promote the fellowship's ends. Members were taught to distrust their own minds, countering any doubts they had about the group or the leader by using a thought-stopping technique called "speaking in tongues."

The Woods thought back to Mona's behavior over the past eight years. They asked themselves if her lack of concern and commitment to social, academic, and vocational endeavors, her inability to make choices, and her emotional withdrawal from family and friends could have been, at least in part, due to the influence of the fellowship. They continued their investigation: "The more information we gathered, the more frightened we became. So frightened, in fact, that we backed off for several months, not wanting to believe that what we were beginning to suspect was true: that Mona was in a destructive cult and was indeed a victim of mind control."

In February of 1981, the Woods invited to their house a young woman who had been a member of the same Bible group as Mona. Carol had left the group voluntarily, but had only been out for a few months. She displayed very little emotion. So little, in fact, that the Woods suspected she was psychologically impaired. The encounter was so upsetting for Mr. Wood that he told his wife firmly, "If this is the end result of getting Mona out of the fellowship, I'm not going to do it."

Carol gave the Woods some articles and told them that the fellowship was psychologically damaging to the members. The Woods asked her, "What are the chances of Mona leaving?" Carol replied, "I don't think there's much of a chance. She's been in too long." Still, Carol advised them to try to get help, and she gave them the names of several people they could call. After Carol left, the Woods agreed that yes, Mona did need help, but that neither of them was ready to employ any type of direct intervention. They both, and especially Mr. Wood, wanted more information.

Over the next two years (1980-1982), the Woods met with various cult experts, mental health professionals, former cult members and their parents, and religious leaders. They amassed a huge amount of information. But what finally persuaded them to take action was a conversation with a priest. Mr. Wood recalls, "He asked us, 'If your daughter had a brain tumor and had one chance in a thousand, would you operate?' And I said of course I would. His reply was, 'Then you have to operate. She's among the living dead right now. You've got to get her out.' "

Although this statement seemed like an exaggeration, the Woods felt a new urgency to help Mona. But they were still plagued by a number of questions: How, exactly, were they to get Mona out of the fellowship? How deeply had she been affected by mind control? What type of help would she need afterwards? Would she hate her parents for trying to get her out? Would she be able to function independently after having spent nearly ten years under mind control?

The Woods carefully researched and evaluated several alternatives for Mona's exit from the fellowship: waiting for Mona to leave on her own; persuading her to go for voluntary counseling; or hiring deprogrammers who would restrain her from leaving until she acknowledged the destructiveness of the group. (They did not consider the option of gaining legal conservatorship over Mona, who was no longer a minor.) In the end, the Woods felt that voluntary counseling would not be feasible, believing Mona's ten-year association with the fellowship would make it impossible for her to be receptive, at least initially, to their plea that she reconsider her commitment to the group.

Most of the parents they had spoken with had advised them that "deprogramming is the only way." After much deliberation the Woods decided that Mona would not cooperate with voluntary counseling, so they chose deprogramming. All things considered, this seemed to be the most effective choice, albeit the most risky.* If the deprogramming failed, for instance, Mona might end up hating

---

* Today, most parents, after educating and preparing themselves as did the Woods, are able to employ voluntary means to persuade their child to reconsider

her parents, and even try to bring charges against them for false imprisonment. And most frightening of all was the risk that the deprogramming might be psychologically harmful to Mona. Although the professionals, parents, former members, and clergy they spoke with seemed to think that eventually Mona would thank her parents for getting her out, regardless of the means they used, the Woods were well aware that there were no guarantees.

The Woods were also troubled by the idea of depriving Mona of her freedom by subjecting her to an involuntary deprogramming. Mona was 28 years old, and what right did they have to impose their values on her? On the other hand, they knew that the fellowship used deceptive, manipulative tactics to recruit and control members: promising peace and love while simultaneously estranging members from their families and friends: withholding information which might cause members to doubt the group; teaching and encouraging the use of mind-controlling techniques which inhibited critical thinking. The Woods concluded that Mona had not been given a chance to make a free, informed choice about joining or not joining the fellowship. She had been an unwitting victim of mind control. Her psychological development was being interrupted, her mind underused, and her energy and good will were being exploited. Therefore, both parents agreed, it was their moral duty to try to deprogram Mona.

The Woods interviewed a number of deprogrammers and former cult members who knew Mona. They wanted someone they could trust and respect, who was familiar with the fellowship's practices and philosophy, and who was gentle and low-key enough to communicate with Mona. They found a man who seemed appropriate, as well as a fomer friend of Mona, and together they set a tentative date for the deprogramming.

The next task facing the Woods was to find adequate post-deprogramming support for Mona, should she decide to leave the fellowship. In response to their questions, one person advised them, "Once she's out, she's yours. Don't worry, though. She'll be fine. You surely don't want to put your daughter in one of those rehabilitation houses with a bunch of sick people." Others strongly recommended finding someone who understood the situation and could be with Mona for a least a month after she left the group, a "counselor-friend" who could encourage and support her through this difficult time, lessening the chances that Mona would drift back into a cult frame of mind and return to the fellowship. The Woods felt more inclined toward this second approach.

Assessing their own situation, the Woods recognized that if Mona did in fact leave the fellowship, she would be returning to a home "where there was nobody

---

a cult involvement, largely because professionals and exit counselors have increased their understanding of the cult phenomenon.

except us. I (Mr. Wood) would be out all day, and I couldn't expect my wife to spend all her time with Mona."

The Woods visited a rehabilitation center whose staff was trained to help former cult members sort through their experiences and reenter mainstream society. Plans were made for Mona to go there after the deprogramming, with the understanding that she would be free to leave at any time.

In addition to making all of these arrangements for Mona, the Woods entered counseling themselves, hoping to learn better ways of communicating with their daughter. Mr. Wood, especially, had been getting into ugly arguments with Mona. The counselor, Ed, advised them to avoid arguing with Mona about the fellowship. Family interactions, he said, should be as pleasant as possible, and communication lines should be kept open at all costs. Ed also suggested trying to remind Mona of the things she missed about home, with the hope that she'd begin asking herself whether she'd rather spend more time with her parents than with the fellowship.

The Woods wrote Mona letters telling her that they were considering selling their beach house, which Mona loved. They said that the upkeep required too much time, money, and physical exertion. Mrs. Wood wrote that her husband wasn't feeling well. Each parent wrote separately, expressing a genuine interest in learning more about her life and telling her how much she was missed. They urged Mona to respond in writing.

Ed also advised the Woods to assume the posture of learners — asking Mona a lot of questions and listening respectfully and attentively to her answers. This approach would provide them, he said, with valuable information about Mona's present state of mind, her feelings about them and about the fellowship, her philosophy of life, and her perception of the world. This "learner" role would also take the Woods out of an adversarial or authoritarian position and therefore make it easier for Mona to trust her parents and accept their sincere love for her.

Finally, Ed told the Woods that they should "allow Mona to be in conflict. Don't try to rescue or protect her from life. Let her experience doubts, ambivalence, uncertainty, confusion. Whatever conflicts she faces," he said, "will keep her mind active and heighten her chances of successfully leaving the fellowship." Mona's parents visited her in a southern state where she had been sent by the fellowship to rent a house, find a job to support herself, and, with four other members, set up a recruitment center and conduct fellowship meetings. During this visit, Mona's parents were struck anew by the difficulty she had in thinking independently, and they urged her to come home for a visit. She said that she wanted to visit them, and a short time later wrote that she would. On her way, however, she stopped at the fellowship's headquarters, and from there called home, in tears, to say that she had changed her mind, adding that she felt she had to follow through on her commitment to the group. Mona's parents felt, from this point, that there was no way they could help her by themselves.

Just prior to the deprogramming date, the Woods went to Mona's graduation from the fellowship university. As they sat among the graduates, listening to long and repetitive lectures, the Woods became painfully aware of the debilitating effects of cults, which until then they had only experienced second-hand through books, articles, and conversations with parents and former cult members. They recalled thinking, "Something is wrong with these beautiful young people." They described "the striking passivity, the absence of critical thought, the submissiveness and uncanny smiles that emanated from these sincere young adults."

It was heartbreaking to realize that their beloved daughter Mona was caught up in this group. And yet, despite their pain, the Woods acknowledged that, "It was a good thing we went out there. As it turned out, the fellowship had warned Mona we might try something, probably deprogramming, to force her to leave the group. Mona had begun to feel suspicious, but our attendance at the graduation allayed her fears and made her feel that we were genuinely interested in what she was doing."

Several weeks after the graduation, Mona came home to visit her parents for a few days. She arrived on Friday. The deprogramming was scheduled for Monday. The Woods took Mona to their beach house for the weekend.

On Monday Mr. Wood picked up the deprogrammers at the airport and dropped them off at the summer home of friends who were travelling abroad and had offered it to the Woods for the deprogramming. Mr. Wood then returned to the beach house, picked up Mona and Mrs. Wood, and set off for the deprogramming site. He drove slowly, carefully, trying not to show the anxiety he was feeling. But Mona hardly noticed. She was relaxed from a weekend at the beach, and looked forward to meeting her parents' friends.

When the Woods arrived at the house, they were greeted by two men and a woman. Mona still unsuspecting, assumed these strangers were her parents' friends, but they were actually security guards who had been hired for the deprogramming. Everyone walked down to the basement, which had been prepared as a bedroom and meeting room for the deprogramming. When they had all gotten downstairs, Mr. Wood turned to his daughter and spoke gently, "Mona, I have something to tell you. You're here because your mother and I want you to hear other opinions and get more information about the fellowship. We're very concerned. We feel you are in a dangerous situation. We are just asking you to listen, to discuss, to try and understand what others know about your group, and then to make up your own mind about whether or not you want to stick with it or leave."

Mona stiffened up immediately, and turned accusingly to the security guards. "You liars! You are kidnapping me! Holding me against my will! I know exactly what you're going to do. You're going to torture me, ruin my relationship with my parents. Well, I am not going to put up with this. I'm leaving right this minute!"

One of the guards turned to Mona and said, "It's your choice, Mona. Either listen or don't listen, but it is to your benefit to listen and get out of here as soon as possible."

Addressing her father, Mona pleaded, "But Dad, they're going to hurt me." "No," Mr. Wood assured her, "we'd never let them hurt you. We'll be here the entire time. Your mother and I will know about everything that is going on."

"Well then," Mona challenged, "go ahead and deprogram me. Where is the deprogrammer, anyway?"* John identified himself as the deprogrammer and said softly, "Mona, we're just going to talk."

Mona, temporarily paralyzed by a rush of feelings, stared at John. She was angry. Angry at her parents for doing this to her. And angry with herself. She never should have come home. She should have believed the fellowship leaders who had warned her not to spend time alone with her parents. But no, she had to do her own thing. How stupid she felt now.

And she was afraid. There was no way of knowing how far these people would go in their attempts to persuade her to leave the fellowship.

And she was confused. John's soft-spoken manner was completely incongruous with her expectations for a deprogrammer.

Mona dashed to the bathroom, trembling, wishing desperately that she could calm down, gather her wits, and come up with a plan for dealing with this crazy situation. Her mother stood outside the unlocked door, trying to console her, but to no avail.

Mona emerged from the bathroom about ten minutes later, clearly shaken. Attempting to sound nonchalant, she told John she would listen to him, considering the fact that she really had no choice. And so the deprogramming began.

---

* Although this is an example of an involuntary deprogramming, it has much in common with voluntary processes. Mona's willingness to challenge the deprogrammers is not atypical, and illustrates why many parents are able to persuade a cult-involved child to talk voluntarily and at length with experts.

That first night everyone was already exhausted from traveling and anxiety, and the discussion, lasting only an hour, focused on explaining the purpose of the deprogramming: to open the mind through reading, discussion, videotapes, films, testimony from ex-fellowship members and from former members of other cults. Mona would be given ample food and rest, she was assured. But she was not free to leave until the deprogrammers felt she was ready.

Not exactly pleased by this restriction, Mona glanced up at the basement windows, which were barred. It was evident that they had taken great precautions against her escaping. "Oh well," she sighed to herself, "I guess I'll be here for awhile."

During the next five days Mona was exposed to information about the fellowship which she had not had access to during her ten years as a loyal member. At first she was very withdrawn, reluctant to enter into debate or discussion, fearful of exposing her own doubts about the fellowship. By the second day, however, Mona's curiosity was aroused by articles describing the techniques of brainwashing used on prisoners of war in China. New thoughts started haunting her: Why did those techniques sound so familiar? Were they used in the fellowship to recruit and indoctrinate members? No. No one had been brainwashed in the fellowship. Everyone was there by choice. Still, the similarities were disquieting: isolation from outside influence; public confession; exclusive vocabulary; polarizing the world into good (the fellowship) and bad (the outside world). Slowly, Mona's resistance gave way to a desire to know, to debate, to discuss, and to ask questions.

Watching a movie about the Nazis, Mona was taken aback by the parallels she saw between the German regime and the fellowship. She recalled the military-type training she had undergone as a group leader, including the riflery practice and instruction in the use of handguns. She wondered whether her group, ostensibly aspiring to love others and to bring peace to the world, was in fact capable of causing harm and committing atrocities.

On the third day a Bible scholar, who was also a former cult member, arrived to explain how the fellowship leader had distorted the scriptures. Mona listened attentively as he spoke. Together they discussed, point by point, how the leader had twisted a word here and there, ever so slightly, to change the meaning of phrases so that the members believed they were following the only true path and that he was the only true interpreter of God's word. After a while, Mona surprised herself by coming up with her own examples.

On the fifth day of the deprogramming Mona tore off the fellowship insignia which she had kept on her Bible, exclaiming, "I won't be needing this anymore! It all makes sense to me now. I can finally see that I've been tricked, seduced, manipulated by the fellowship. It almost destroyed my feelings for my parents. It kept me from really growing up, from experiencing real life, from having relationships with people, and from caring about the world. I'm NOT going back there!"

Mr. and Mrs. Wood looked at each other and heaved an enormous sigh of relief. "Yes," they acknowledged silently, "Mona has come a long way." At the same time, both of them knew there were still some very difficult months ahead.

The following day everyone departed and Mr. and Mrs. Wood took Mona to the airport where all three boarded a plane for the rehabilitation center. Her parents were concerned that Mona might have "flashbacks" and try to return to the group. Two counselors from the center met her at the arrival gate, and the three of them drove for about a half hour to a large house bordered by pine trees on a quiet street. Mona spent several weeks at the center, gathering information, talking to many former cult members, and trying to get accustomed to having — and enjoying — leisure time. It was a stimulating, enriching, informative three weeks. Her parents came up for a weekend of family counseling, which was healing for all of them. By the time Mona left she felt ready to face the world. There was a whole life, she realized, her own life, to be lived. And this was a new beginning.

Mona spent the next month helping out on other deprogrammings. She was constantly on the move, talking about her own experience of having been manipulated and controlled by a cult. She exulted in her new understanding, in her new freedom to make choices, to have friends, and to live her own life.

After one month as a deprogrammer, Mona decided it was time she returned home to her parents and started focusing on her post-cult life. She needed to figure out where she was going to live and what type of work she wanted to do. These were big life choices, and, suddenly, freedom seemed overwhelming. Mona felt inept, confused, despondent. Ten years had elapsed while she had been in a cult. She was 29, supposedly an adult, and yet she felt so immature, as though she were just graduating from high school. Had those years been totally wasted? Had she grown, matured, learned anything during that time?

Mona was ashamed, lonely, disappointed in herself; reluctant to let her parents know how deeply depressed she was. She didn't want them to baby her or be worried or disappointed. So she cried herself to sleep at night, wondering whether there really was a God, or a true purpose in life. Mornings were especially difficult, waking up to empty, unplanned days, spending meaningless hours, looking at a near-stranger in the mirror, feeling acutely vulnerable and insecure.

Mona knew she really needed help. But she didn't know whom to ask. And she didn't know whom to trust. But with the help of former cult members, counselors, and friends, as well as time and the continuing support of her parents, Mona was in the end able to come to grips with what had happened to her and create for herself a normal and mature existence.

Mr. and Mrs. Wood watched Mona struggle. They stood by her, day after day, wishing it were easier, wishing they could do more, wishing they didn't feel so helpless...

Today, Mona is in the real estate business. She still resents the time lost in the fellowship, and feels ten years "behind schedule." But she experiences the laughter, joy, struggle, and pain of normal life, and now makes her own decisions.

Chapter Two

Destructive Cults

General Characteristics

Definitions. The term "cult" has often been used to denote a group whose beliefs and practices are shrouded in secrecy and exclusivity, which differs significantly from established religions, and whose members congregate around a specific deity or person. Throughout history, cultists have been labeled as religious extremists, heretics, and social deviants by mainstream society.

Over the past fifteen years there has been a significant rise in the number, size, and influence of cults, and the word "cult" itself has taken on an increasingly sinister connotation, evoking such images as parents estranged from their children, impoverished followers devoted to an opulent, "God-inspired" leader, and sharp, intelligent minds turned to jelly after being subjected to a variety of clever and all-too-successful brainwashing techniques. Indeed, a large body of evidence indicates that many contemporary cults have had harmful effects both on their members and on society at large.

One such example of harm was tragically provided by the People's Temple cult, with the November, 1978 deaths of more than 900 followers of Jim Jones during a cult death ritual at Jonestown, Guyana. This incident brought cults keenly into public awareness, prompting cult education programs and increased media coverage of the more notorious groups.

After Jonestown, parents who had previously dismissed the cult issue as "irrelevant" began to worry about their sons and daughters. A teenager's affiliation with radical or off-beat groups, once tolerated by parents as part of their child's growing up, now set off fears that "it might be a cult."

Parents' concern is augmented by uncertainty, because not all radical groups are cults, and not all cultic groups are destructive. In fact, a pluralistic society such as ours is committed to tolerate, support, and even encourage groups reflecting a wide range of lifestyles, beliefs, and practices. To condemn any group simply because it is different would be a promotion of intolerance, discrimination, even oppression. Therefore, one must look beyond appearance to determine whether or not a group is destructive.

Destructive[*] cults are those which tend to use extreme and unethical techniques of manipulation to recruit and assimilate members and to control members' thoughts, feelings, and behavior as a means of furthering the leader's goals. Although most cults that have aroused concern are religious, they can also be political, commercial, or pseudotherapeutic.

The leaders of such groups often claim divinity or superhuman powers. They often demand childlike obedience and subservience from their followers. They encourage inordinate dependency in members for guidance not only in spiritual matters, but in other areas as well — ranging from inconsequential practical decisions (for example, "What toothbrush should I use?") to personal and intimate choices ("Whom shall I marry?"), from codes of morality (Is it okay to steal for God?") to political choices ("For whom shall I vote?")

Destructive cults espouse and enforce beliefs and practices which converts are told are absolutely true, above secular law, and vital to salvation, happiness, fulfillment, etc.. With an ostensible purpose to spread love and peace to the world, they often perpetuate a highly intolerant "we-they" mentality. The typical result is a paranoid view of the non-cult world, and guarded, manipulative interactions with outsiders.

In destructive cults, individuality is superseded by the collective group interests. Converts are pressured to modify their personalities to conform to the group's ideal. Intimacy between members, and especially with non-members, is restricted and tightly controlled, often resulting in stilted relationships and an overall absence of warmth. Although sexual relationships are encouraged in some cults and prohibited in others, the group's interest, and not personal fulfillment, is often the determining factor.

Mental health professionals, clergy, physicians, parents, and former members have spoken out about the drastic and destructive personality changes they have witnessed in many converts. In addition to inflicting harm on their members, these cults have been associated with the breaking up of families (for example, through divorce, child custody battles, and lawsuits pitting parents against their own children), and have been known to engage in deceptive and unlawful practices that violate the very fabric of our democratic society.

How Cults May Differ

Size. Cult size may range from groups of 3 or 4 to groups with thousands of members.

---

* Although we have placed the adjective "destructive" in front of "cult" in order to emphasize that some cults are benign, we, like most writers in this field, will use the word "cult" with the pejorative connotations of "destructive" implied.

Language. Different groups use different "buzz words," that is, vocabulary which has a special, exclusive meaning to members and which would not be understood by outsiders.

Scripture or prescriptive text. Some cults publish their own holy book(s), manual(s), and inspirational writings. Others claim to base their teachings on a traditional scripture such as the Bible, but actually modify, distort, plagiarize, misinterpret, or quote such scripture out of context in a way that promotes the group's views. Finally, there are the eclectic cults which claim to represent the fulfillment of all religious prophecies and draw their inspirational material from a variety of religious, mystical, and occult writings.

Leader. Most cult leaders are male, although some are female. They may be young (Guru Maharaj Ji of the Divine Light Mission started out as the 8-year-old Perfect Master) or old, and come from various religious, cultural, educational, and socio-economic backgrounds.

Lifestyle. Cult dress varies from the ordinary to the exotic. Diet may be strictly vegetarian, dangerously bizarre, or normal. In some cults communal living is required, while in others the majority of members live on their own. Sexual norms vary, with some groups espousing celibacy and others promoting free sex as a means of achieving higher consciousness. Recruitment and fund-raising activities are emphasized in many cults, but in other groups most members have jobs in the "outside world."

Financial obligations may be explicit, requiring members to give anywhere from 10% to 100% of their earnings, savings, and material assets to the group. Or, members may be encouraged or pressured into taking increasingly expensive courses sponsored by the cult. Other groups exploit members financially by requiring them to donate free labor (often described as "service" to the Lord, guru, master, or whatever title is assumed by the leader.).

Destructive Cult Ideology

Despite the great variations among cults, certain common themes stand out:

Submission to leadership. Even if the leader makes major changes in the specific ideology, followers are expected to adjust their views accordingly, thus demonstrating their faith in the leader.

Polarized world view. The cult is good, the outside world is bad.

Feeling over thought. Emotions, gut feelings, intuition, and the like are regarded as more credible than rational conclusions.

Manipulation of feelings by the leader and other members.

Denigration of critical thinking, characterizing the mind, rational thought, and intellectual activities as extraneous or evil.

Salvation, fulfillment, and/or self-realization only through conforming to the group.

Ends justify means. Any action is acceptable so long as it promotes the group's goals.

Group over individual. The group's concerns supersede the individual's concerns, goals, aspirations, and needs.

Secrecy, elitism, guarded initiation rites.

Warnings of severe or supernatural sanctions for defection from the cult.

Severing of ties with past: family, friends, goals, interests.

Group beliefs constitute the absolute truth and are above secular law.

Group membership gives one access to special powers and privileges.

Categories

For purposes of identification, we have divided (destructive) cults into a few rough categories, described below.

Eastern meditation. In these groups the leader's background is often in Eastern philosophy and religion, for example, Buddhism, Hinduism, Sikhism. Eastern scriptures such as the Bhagavad Gita are plagiarized and reinterpreted to justify and aggrandize the leader, who is often regarded as God incarnate. Beliefs held by these groups may include: one can achieve God-consciousness, become one with God, merge with God, often through meditation; one should become detached from personal thoughts and feelings, and worldly aspirations; the material world is an illusion; reincarnation occurs at death.

Bible-based-Christian. In these groups the Bible is exploited to support the group's views, and the leader is often regarded as a prophet of God, if not the second coming of Jesus. Members often believe that faith in the leader will result in salvation, that Armageddon is imminent, and that they must learn to suppress their doubts and criticisms of the group by speaking in tongues, chanting, and prayer.

Occult, satanist, witchcraft, black magic. These groups use exotic ritual in an attempt to harness supernatural powers. They are often characterized by intense secrecy, exclusivity, and in some cases by the worship of Satan or the Antichrist.

Political-terrorist. These groups may be secular, or based in Eastern or Western philosophy or religion. They believe that their purpose is to overthrow "evil" governments or other institutions, and they feel justified in using terrorist tactics to further their cause. Members are often required to undergo paramilitary training.

Psychotherapy/human potential. These groups use psychological terminology to promote their legitimacy. They offer such attractions as instant cures for mental distress, the promise of gaining total control over one's life, the ability to manipulate others for personal gain; unlimited access to one's creative capacities, and self-realization. The leader is often revered as a super-therapist with special powers. Members may be subjected to intensive encounter-type sessions geared to lowering their defenses, providing an emotional "high," and creating a fierce loyalty to the group's philosophy and leader.

Drug and alcohol abuse programs. Under the guise of substance abuse treatment programs, these groups often subject members to strong verbal abuse, a highly regimented and sometimes militaristic lifestyle, and forced displays of subservience and obedience to the leader.

Commercial. These groups promise quick, easy, sizeable earnings (or even instant wealth) to anyone and everyone who dedicates himself to the sale of their products. Members are often encouraged to use deception as they sell and recruit others to sell. Many are left more destitute than when they started, because the investment required is more than they can possibly afford, and the commission they receive is significantly smaller than what they were promised.

Why People Join Cults: Cult Tactics

Membership in a destructive cult is the result of two interacting forces: (1) the tactics the cult uses to recruit, convert, acculturate, and hold members, and (2) the personal vulnerability of the potential recruit. We will first examine the role cults play in attracting and maintaining members.

Recruitment Tactics

Cult recruiters, skilled in evaluating likely prospects, will often seek out travelers, distressed individuals, those in transitional situations (such as college students), elderly persons, and naive teenagers, all of whom are likely to be hungry for friendliness and warmth and looking for affiliations. Although specific tactics vary, certain common features are noted below.

Once a prospect seems receptive, the recruiter makes a **calculated** effort to engage him in conversation, spark his interest, and capture his full attention by:

Showing concern for the prospect's well being, expressing a presumptuous familiarity with his feelings and emotional state which makes the prospect believe he is truly understood. For example, upon learning about a potential convert's travels, a recruiter might say, "So, you've been on the road for two months. You must feel kind of tired, lonely, without any real roots?"

Demonstrating acute, shared interest in the prospect's ideas, interests, hopes, goals, by saying, for example, "Oh, you're a musician. Well, I just happen to live with a group of musicians..."

Holding eye contact, maintaining close physical proximity, "coming on" sexually.

Extracting personal information about the prospect's current situation and concerns, problems, stresses. For example, a recruiter might ask, "What do your parents think about your cross-country travels?", or, "Are you involved in an intimate relationship with someone?", or "Do you know what you want to do with your life?"

If the recruiter is successful, the prospect will feel an emotional bond with the recruiter, along with a willingness or desire to maintain contact.

When prospects are deemed ready — and this may be after a fifteen minute conversation or after several encounters — they may then be invited to join or visit the group. Recruiters will often tailor their descriptions of the group to match the interests of the prospect. For example, a prospect looking for spiritual fulfillment may be invited to a "spiritual discussion group," while the same recruiter might invite a prospect interested in psychology to a "human potential workshop."

To the naive or uninformed observer, cult recruiters appear to be very concerned about an individual's well-being. However, their true intent is much less admirable — to quickly assess whether the prospect would be an asset to the group, that is, able to bring in money and new members. If deemed a worthwhile "investment," the prospect will be showered with attention and lavish concern until he makes a commitment to join the group. At that point, the initial concern of the recruiter is refocused on other likely candidates. Unfortunately, the new recruit is often too consumed by enthusiasm for his new allegiance to notice that his good buddy the recruiter has deserted him for somebody else.

Note: Different cults use different techniques of recruitment, while some exclusive cults pay little attention to recruitment. The above is a very general and somewhat sketchy description. Also, please note that many popular therapies, and even some traditional religions offer promises of fulfillment similar to those offered by destructive cults. However, destructive cults can be distinguished by their totalitarian structure, their unconscionable manipulation, and by the resulting harm inflicted on members.

Conversion
The goal of conversion in destructive cults is to ensure that a prospect unconditionally adopts the beliefs, practices, and personality traits prescribed by the group.

The length of time involved in conversion varies from one prospect to the next, and from group to group. Some cults attempt to effect a complete conversion during an intensive weekend; others have a more subdued approach, whetting the appetites of potential converts over a period of weeks or months before allowing them to be initiated formally into the group.

Some individuals are never completely converted. These people remain on the fringes of the group, are considered part-timers, and never attain high status among the members. Partial or unsuccessful conversion may be due to inability to conform to group expectations, an unusual capacity to resist group pressure, boredom, or non-cult commitments or responsibilities which prove too attractive and/or demanding for even the high pressure persuasion of a cult.

Successful conversion is often accompanied by a radical change in converts, as they take on the cult's ideal personality (acceding to the cult's demand that they "Become like a child," "Become completely peaceful," "Be detached from the material world," and the like), and replace their previous lifestyle, vocabulary, interests, friends, and values with those prescribed by the cult. This dramatic split from the past may initially cause great stress for converts, who often feel torn between their past and present lives, pulled by conflicting allegiances, and confused about their true identities. Continued conformity to cult practices and beliefs, however, often relieves this stress, and eventually prior beliefs, lifestyles, and even past experiences seem distant, partly forgotten, and essentially dissociated from day-to-day consciousness.

Although the specifics may vary from group to group, there are a number of common tactics used by destructive cults to effect conversion. Some of these include:

Control of time and activities, that is, subjecting potential converts to a calculated, rigorous time schedule, within which every moment is taken up with physically and emotionally strenuous activities. This leaves little or no time for privacy and reflection. Such a schedule might include: marathon lectures, prolonged encounter group sessions, intense one-on-one counseling, wild dancing or vigorous sports, hypnotic exercises, visualizations, meditations, chanting, fervent prayer sessions, inadequate sleep and food.

Effects: lowered psychological defense, narrowed attention, physical and emotional exhaustion, impaired ability to critically evaluate the group, trance-like states which are often exhilarating and which render one extremely suggestible.

Information control, for example: cutting off or denigrating outside sources of information such as television, radio, newspapers, communication with outsiders; bombarding prospects with cult literature, tapes, and indoctrination lectures; classifying certain information about the cult as "secret," (for example, who the leader is; what sacrifices, lifestyle changes, and financial obligations are required of members; where the money goes); misrepresentation ("We're collecting money for disadvantaged children") and outright lies ("None of our members gives money to the leader." "We don't believe our guru is God.").

Effects: Information control precludes informed decision-making and therefore prevents critical evaluation of the cult.

Language manipulation. This may be accomplished by ascribing new meanings or connotations to ordinary words. For example, in the Divine Light Mission, the word "knowledge" means the four techniques of meditation taught during the initiation session which supposedly gives one knowledge of God; the word "mind" is synonymous with the evil thoughts and forces inside people that lead them away from God and Truth; "the world" refers to that which is outside of Divine Light Mission and therefore unenlightened. Additional tactics include: use of exclusive vocabulary (for example, made-up words and phrases); introduction of foreign language(s) in conversation and song; discouraging "trite" conversation about non-cult activities, interests, and ideas; belittling the expression of personal thoughts and feelings about one's past and future.

Effects: Prospects feel privy to exclusive language and vocabulary and new knowledge. They come to feel more comfortable communicating with cult members, and eventually, once the language becomes part of their everyday speech, feel inhibited in their communication with outsiders, who obviously cannot understand. This contributes to a polarized "we-they" mentality with potential converts beginning to identify more with the cult and less with the non-cult world.

Discouraging critical, rational thought. For example, many cults dismiss members' doubts, criticisms, and questions with statements like,

"Everything will become clear in time," or with threats like, "Satan is at the root of all doubt," or with exhortations like, "If you want to know God, you must reach beyond rationality."

Effects: Prospects feel guilty for doubting, questioning, or using their intellectual abilities to evaluate the cult. Many even come to regard their minds as troublemakers, generators of poisonous doubts, tools of Satan, and the like.

Instruction in trance-induction techniques. These may include: meditation, chanting, speaking in tongues, self-hypnosis, visualization, and controlled breathing exercises.

Effects: These techniques, especially if revealed to converts during intense, exclusive, initiation ceremonies, often make converts feel privy to special and/or divine powers. Trance induction and the like can be very useful in suppressing doubts and in increasing suggestibility to further indoctrination. In some especially vulnerable people, use of such techniques may contribute to psychotic breakdowns.

Confession sessions, during which members are pressured to reveal extremely personal information about past and present transgressions and sins, whether real or imagined.

Effects: Prospects who reveal such information may feel an initial sense of guilt and shame, and then a sense of relief at having confessed. They may even become dependent on this self-denigrating activity as a means of relieving guilt. However, those who want to leave the cult are often fearful that the cult may use the information they have revealed to blackmail or slander them.

Group pressure, that is, offering positive reinforcement such as approval, affection, or raised status when members agree with group goals, and withholding such reinforcement or punishing those who speak or act against cult prescriptions.

Effect: Prospects may succumb to group pressure despite strongly held convictions that conflict with cult beliefs and practices.

Maintaining converts' loyalty

Destructive cults recognize that even the most dedicated converts are susceptible to doubts and may even defect unless they are subjected to an intensive and ongoing maintenance program. Therefore, much time and effort is put into maintaining converts' loyalty, using tactics such as those described below.

Persuade convert to maintain a rigorous lifestyle which reflects cult values. Many cults operate communal houses where all activities center around cult goals. Pressure to live in these houses is often exerted on members through promises of higher status, for example, "Guru loves all his children, but he especially loves those who join his monastic house and dedicate their entire lives to him."

Effects: Adhering to a cult lifestyle serves to confirm and reinforce a convert's commitment to cult beliefs. In addition, arduous schedules of fund-raising, recruitment, and other cult-oriented activities leave converts exhausted, without time or energy to question cult beliefs.

Instruction in, and excessive use of trance-induction techniques such as meditation, prayer, chanting, self-hypnosis, and speaking in tongues.

Effects: Such techniques may result in: suppression of thoughts, feelings, and doubts; impaired intellectual and critical capacity; occasionally, psychopathology. Note: These techniques are not in themselves harmful. They cause harm because they are used to suppress, rather than understand and "work through" mental difficulties.

Public testimony of loyalty, such as: encouraging new converts to recruit others (some cults offer high status and other rewards to successful recruiters), to testify at public meetings, to sign statements of loyalty.

Effects: Public testimony reinforces converts' commitment to the cult and makes leaving appear to be a betrayal of trust.

Repeated threats of sanctions for leaving, such as: "If you leave, your life will fall apart;" or, "your soul will rot;" or "you will go to hell;" or, "your relatives will suffer;" or, "your life will be in danger."

Effect: Converts become afraid to leave the cult.

The promise of imminent fulfillment, peace, salvation, for example, telling converts that if they "just try a little harder, give a little more" of themselves, they will attain whatever reward the cult has promised.

Effects: Converts are continually striving to attain utopian ideals, and blame themselves for not trying hard enough.

Limited or no access to outside sources of information.

Effect: No contrasting views to stimulate critical thinking about the cult. Reinforcement of notion that doubts about the group reflect defects in the doubter, not the group.

Absence of non-cult relationships and emotional support.

Effects: Converts become dependent on the cult for friendship, intimacy, and emotional support; feelings of alienation, hostility, and paranoia towards the non-cult world are further reinforced.

Control of sexuality and intimacy within the cult; for example, the leader may dictate whether, when, and whom to marry, whether and when to have sexual relations, children, sterilization, abortion.

Effects: Converts may develop a distorted, impersonal view of sexuality and intimacy. The leadership is protected from the possibility of intimates' sharing and reinforcing doubts about the group.

Ongoing confession and self-denigration.

Effects: Converts feel ashamed, then relieved, then indebted to the cult for saving them from their "evil nature."

Excessive financial obligations, often requiring the signing over of inheritances, bank accounts, paychecks, and other material assets (such as cars and stereos) to the cult.

Effects: Members are left virtually penniless and financially dependent on the group. Also, if a lot of money has been donated, converts may justify their investment by blinding themselves to the destructive aspects of the group.

Why People Join Cults: Personal Vulnerability

In the previous pages we explored some of the tactics used by cults to recruit, convert, and hold members. But not everyone who is approached by a cult recruiter becomes a member. Some people seem to be more vulnerable than others.

Although there is no one personality profile for cult members, there are certain factors which affect a person's vulnerability to recruitment, including stage of development, situational factors, personal background, and psychological predispositions.

Stage of Development
Many teenagers and young adults are relatively free of serious responsibilities and commitments such as having a family or a full time job. Their lack of experience in the world is often accompanied by naiveté and idealism, leaving them open to the inflated promises and simplistic answers offered by cults.

But adolescents are not the only vulnerable population. Elderly people may also be ripe for cult recruitment. For example, older people living alone, many of whose friends have died or moved away, may welcome the apparent warmth, interest, and companionship offered by cult recruiters. Likewise, the disabled and infirm may gratefully open their doors to recruiters who offer to clean their houses, cook their meals, do their grocery shopping, and chat for hours over a cup of tea. And retired people, looking for new ways to engage themselves in life, may be lured by the cults' group activities and the renewed sense of purpose and idealism.

Many cults have taken advantage of elderly members, who have relatively few commitments or responsibilities and plenty of time to donate to the group. In addition, the elderly are targeted for their social security checks, their material assets, their wills, etc.

In recent years, cults have allotted much time and energy to recruitment campaigns in such retirement areas as Florida, Arizona, and California. Unfortunately, they have been quite successful — many elderly have been buying the cults' promises and signing over their possessions. Without friends or relatives to help them, they have little chance of escaping from the cult environment. Moreover, those who attempt to leave may be frightened into staying by threats from the group.

Situational Factors
People who are going through a particularly stressful time in their lives (for example, the death of a loved one, divorce, unemployment, moving, going away to college, severe illness, prison, military service, debilitation due to aging or disease), may be more vulnerable to the promises of happiness and relief from suffering offered by cults. Those experiencing such troubled transitions may feel that their way of operating in the world isn't working, and, therefore, are open to recruiters selling "happiness."

Personal Background

Socio-economic background. Young people growing up in poor neighborhoods often develop "street smarts" that alert them to the ploys of hustlers, smiling strangers, and so-called free lunches. Cynicism, suspicion, and keen survival instincts often render these youngsters less vulnerable to cults than their middle and upper income counterparts, who often have had little or no exposure to such exploitative elements. (Although, in many ways, delinquent gangs may function like cults for these youths.)

Certain cults, however, concentrate on recruiting poor and/or homeless people, promising to fulfill their material and spiritual needs, while simultaneously stealing their welfare checks, foster care payments, social security benefits, etc., and forcing them to work without pay for the cults.

Education. Many cults do their major recruiting at colleges. Some cults have even registered as legitimate student organizations and are authorized to use meeting rooms, offices, and sometimes even housing facilities on campus. College students, especially those living on campus, are likely to be approached by cult recruiters.

High schools, too, have been infiltrated by cults. Some groups have run formal programs that were actually approved by uninformed school administrations. Other cults approach students before and after school or between classes.

Certain cults encourage their members to become certified elementary school teachers so that they might have an influence on the youngsters during their formative years.

Fortunately, many educators have become aware of cult dangers and are currently arranging cult education programs for their students.

Religious background. Contrary to popular belief, formal religious training has not proved to be a fail-safe deterrent to cult recruitment, although religious background may influence the type of cult to which a person is vulnerable.

Christian vulnerability: A number of cults have infiltrated and, on more than one occasion, taken over entire churches. This process often begins with cult members' becoming teachers in church religious schools, becoming active on church committees, and eventually rising to leadership positions within the congregation. In this way, practicing Christians may be unwittingly recruited into cults (often labeled "pseudo-Christian" or "shepherding/discipleship" cults).

Jewish vulnerability: Certain Hebrew Christian cults are committed to recruiting and converting Jews to Christianity, using deceptive tactics to accomplish their goal. Many of these groups use Jewish symbols, terminology, rituals, and scripture to lure unsuspecting prospects to their version of Sabbath services, Passover seders, etc., where slowly and subtly they introduce the idea of Jesus as Lord of the Jews. Some Hebrew Christian cults have sent representatives to Israel where they concentrate their recruiting efforts on young travelers who have gone to Israel seeking spiritual fulfillment and a stronger Jewish identity.

Family Dynamics
The degree of closeness, the frequency and quality of communication, and the type of power structure (e.g., authoritarian or democratic) among family members may detract from or contribute to a person's vulnerability to cults. However, cult members come from both solid "happy" families and broken, unstable homes.

Psychological Predispositions
Certain cult tactics are similar, if not identical to, techniques used by hypnotists. Some of these include a soothing, singsong tone of voice; close physical proximity and touch; prolonged eye contact; repetition of short catch phrases; suggesting that the subject relax, open up, trust, etc. Consequently, good hypnotic subjects may also be highly susceptible to cult recruiters.

People suffering from some type of psychological disorder and those taking drugs (prescription or non-prescription) may also be very suggestible and thus prime targets.

The majority of cultists are relatively normal persons made vulnerable from stress and/or certain personality traits, among which are dependency needs, unassertiveness, gullibility, low tolerance for ambiguity, cultural disillusionment, naive idealism, undiscerning desire for spiritual meaning, susceptibility or attraction to trance-like states, and ignorance of the ways in which groups can manipulate individuals.

It is important to recognize that no matter how healthy, well-educated, or happy a person may be, everyone experiences some degree of frustration, mood fluctuation, and vulnerability. No one is immune from loneliness, emotional fatigue, grief, despair, idealism, and naivete. We must conclude, therefore, that there is no guaranteed immunity from destructive cults.

Harmful Effects

The following is a list of harms caused by cults. It is important to note, however, that each cult is different. Some are more harmful than others, depending on their particular power structure, philosophy, environment, practices, and leader. All of these factors, and the particular characteristics of the convert, need to be considered in evaluating a cult's potential to harm a particular person.

Potential Harm to Members

Physical harm.
- Increased susceptibility to accidents, illness, and general fatigue.
- Nutritional deficiencies.
- (In cults where promiscuity and/or prostitution are the norms) increased exposure to sexually-transmitted diseases.
- Beatings, especially of children.
- Sexual abuse, especially of women and children.
- Unnecessary death due to inadequate medical attention.

Financial harm. Financial dependence on the cult leaves members with no recourse in case of medical or other emergencies. Should they want to leave, members often don't have the money to do so. Finally, if they manage to leave (with outside assistance, for example), they may not have the resources to support themselves in the non-cult world. Many wealthy members have turned over enormous trust funds to cults.

Psychological harm. Loss of autonomy, diminished ability to make decisions and critical judgments (especially in groups where members rely on their superiors or the leader to make ethical and practical decisions such as whether to get married, quit a job, go to college, visit parents, etc. This kind of harm is also likely where there is limited or no access to outside sources of information).

- Maturational arrest (for example, a 30-year-old who has never dated because of cult proscriptions).
- Mental disturbances such as: hallucinations, distorted perceptions of reality, split personality, nervous breakdowns, psychotic episodes, paranoia, delusions of grandeur, regression to childlike behavior, suicidal thinking (these symptoms are more likely to occur in groups which advocate extensive use of thought-stopping techniques).
- Radical personality changes.
- Impaired psychological integration, that is, dissociation from pre-cult family, heritage, friends, values, and personality, and from future goals. Members may strive to exist in a narrow, one-dimensional present, denying the past and the future.
- Alienation, hostility, paranoia, and apathy toward mainstream society.
- Impaired capacity for independent critical thinking.

Potential Harm to Families

Emotional harm. Parents, siblings, and spouses of cult members are often distraught over the changes a cult has wrought in their loved one. They may feel additional frustration if the cult limits contact or communication between members and their families (such as discouraging or prohibiting visits home). Separation and divorce, child custody disputes, and serious emotional problems within families have erupted as a result of cult stresses.

Financial harm. Cult members may pressure or deceive their families into donating a great deal of money to the group. Also, trying to help a cult member leave the group can prove to be an expensive endeavor.

Physical harm. Some cults have gone so far as to threaten or cause physical harm to families who oppose them.

Wider Social Harm
Touting the absolute righteousness of their cause, cults breed hostility and disregard for the values, institutions, laws, property, and cultural norms of mainstream society. As a result of their cult training, members often feel they have the right to engage in fraudulent or even destructive activities — ranging from deceptive solicitation to actually inflicting harm on those the cult labels as "enemies."

In essence, cults can rob their members of conscience, stripping away feelings of responsibility toward the "outside world" and minimizing the value of an individual life to the point where some members are willing to take their own or others' lives for the "cause."

Chapter Three

The Parents' Experience

Parents often recognize a problem with their children long before it becomes noticeable to the rest of the world. Years of living with, loving, nurturing, and watching a child grow, endow parents with an intuitive sense about their children to which no one else is privy. Therefore, the parent who says, "Something is wrong with my child," deserves to be taken seriously.

It is unfortunate that parents who go for counseling regarding their child are often inaccurately labeled as "worrywarts," "overprotective," or "having some deep-rooted psychological problems of their own." This blanket dismissal of concerned parents is unfair and presumptuous. Saddest of all, it can and often does discourage them from trusting their own rational judgment and intuition, and hinders them from getting the information and support they need to help their child.

The fact is, the parents who come to us for counseling are, for the most part, responding to very real, specific, observable, and often sudden behavior changes which they can't explain and which prompt fears that their child is in trouble and may be caught off guard.

In counseling these parents we treat each case individually, taking into consideration each family's unique history and particular strengths and limitations. However, after working with hundreds of families, we and our colleagues have noted a number of thoughts, feelings, and behavioral reactions which are commonly observed in parents, and which we have attempted to highlight in this chapter.

Our intentions are twofold: first, to help parents identify, better understand, and gain some distance from their experiences, so that they can make clearer, more rational decisions as they attempt to help their child; second, to help parents recognize that although they may feel isolated and overwhelmed by their situation, they are not alone in their thoughts, feelings, and behavioral reactions to sudden changes in their child.

Behavior that Worries Parents

In recounting their experiences, a good many parents attribute their initial worry or concern to sudden, often radical changes in a son's or daughter's behavior. Below are some of the more common changes (which do *not necessarily* imply a cult involvement) reported to us by parents.

Secretive behavior. "My son insists on speaking privately with his friends. He refuses to tell me where he's going. He acts like he's doing something wrong. He withholds information and sometimes even lies to me, which is so uncharacteristic of him. He resents being asked questions about his activities, his feelings, or his plans for the immediate or long-range future. He isolates himself in his room, guarding his privacy and his possessions tenaciously. He never used to be this way."

Change in vocabulary or speech patterns. "Our daughter used to be a great communicator — so expressive, so articulate, so creative with words. Suddenly, it's as though a completely different person is talking to us. Her speech is slow and deliberate. It lacks color and imagination. The expressions, the vocabulary, just aren't hers. Our conversations are like dead ends. If we challenge her, she spouts platitudes and generalizations. Sometimes it seems as though she's speaking from a memorized script."

Emotional changes. "Our warm, engaging son has done an about-face. He treats us as though we were distant acquaintances. Whereas before he was the first to open his arms for a hug, now he virtually recoils at any display of affection. When we asked him if anything was wrong he simply shrugged his shoulders and said, 'Let's face it, we have different interests in life.' Occasionally he'll send us a birthday card signed 'love, John,' but it feels so forced, so unspontaneous, as though he's trying to prove that he cares."

Shift in friends and activities. "Our son suddenly lost interest in all his old buddies and started associating with a new group of friends. They don't go out — no movies, no dancing, no restaurants. Instead, they have very serious, exclusive meetings at one another's homes. We don't know much about them because they keep to themselves. We don't mind being outsiders, but we're worried about our son."

Rejection of secular goals. "Our daughter has always been a bright student. It doesn't make sense to us that she dropped out of college in her junior year. She explained it by saying, 'Secular education isn't important to me anymore,' but we still don't understand why."

Dubious financial activities. "Our son has always been good with money. As a teenager, he saved almost everything he made, and later on used the money in responsible ways. Suddenly it seems as though he's lost all sense of financial responsibility — giving away more than he can afford to some religious organization we've never heard of before; pressuring us to cash in his life insurance policy and give him whatever money we might have left to him in our will; not paying his bills; using credit cards as though they offered him unlimited funds. We just don't understand what's come over him."

Disturbing sexual attitudes. "In both high school and college our daughter was popular with men, and she has always expressed an interest in getting married and having a family. But for several months now she hasn't been dating anyone and she tells us she's no longer interested in finding a partner or having children."

Abrupt marital decisions. "Our son has always been very selective in choosing his friends and girlfriends. And yet, after joining some spiritual commune, he married a woman he had known for only two weeks! We can't understand it." *Or*, "Our daughter was happily married with three children and a bright, sensitive husband. Suddenly, one week after she attended a weekend therapy workshop, she announced that she was filing for a divorce. It's very upsetting to all of us."

Shifts in religious, philosophical, or political views. "We raised our son as a practicing, committed Jew. Now he absolutely refuses to attend services. Instead, he lights incense, meditates in front of a picture of an Indian guru, and reads book after book about Eastern religions. It's all very strange to us."

Extreme commitments. "Our daughter started selling health products about a month ago as a means of earning some extra money. But suddenly it seems as though it's become her whole life. She goes to meetings four nights a week and incentive workshops twice a month. She tries to pressure us into buying her products, and insists that these health goods will change our lives for the better. Several of her friends have called us because they're worried that she's getting too entrenched in this commercial endeavor."

Unconventional lifestyle. "After living alone for several years, our son moved into a communal house. It seems strange to us — men and women living together, unmarried, following a strict vegetarian diet, and sharing living expenses. Although the house is clean, there is very little furniture and most of the residents sleep on mats on the floor."

Changes in appearance. "Our son was always very casual about his appearance. We used to complain about his scraggly beard and loose-fitting old clothes. But now we're a little uncomfortable with his abrupt switch to a clean-shaven, well-dressed look. It seems unnatural for him. And the young people he's been associating with all dress the same way. It's almost like a uniform."

Vocational turnabouts. "After rising to a high management position in a successful computer company, our daughter suddenly decided to abandon her career. She now works on an assembly line in a paper factory, which she says she prefers because 'it takes less concentration.' "

Indications of psychological distress. "Our daughter used to be busy all the time. Now she sleeps until noon. Even then, she has trouble facing the day. She talks about life being meaningless. She's afraid people know what she's thinking. She told us she hears voices when she's alone."

Diminished academic performance. "Our son was getting straight A's in college, but this semester he failed two of his courses and barely passed the others."

Common Thoughts and Feelings

Observing the behavior described above can evoke troubling thoughts and feelings in parents, as evidenced in the following themes frequently observed in counseling sessions:

Guilt. "What did we do wrong? Why didn't we recognize it sooner?"

Shame, embarrassment, self-consciousness. "What will other people (for example, relatives, colleagues, friends, neighbors, strangers) think when they see our daughter behaving this way?"

Fear. "Is it too late to help? Is it something that can be corrected, or has our child been permanently damaged?"

Accusations.
Blame Child. "She never did anything right."
Blame Others. "It's my husband's (wife's) fault. He (she) was too permissive (strict) with our children."

Bitterness toward life, God, fate. "Why is this happening to us? We didn't do anything to deserve it. Life is so terribly unfair."

Loneliness. "I wish I had somebody to talk to, someone who cares, someone who understands."

Anger. "I'd like to strangle the people who did this to my son."

Sense of being burdened, overwhelmed. "We put in 25 long hard years raising our son, supporting him financially all the way through graduate school, and helping out emotionally when he needed us. But now we're tired. We need a rest. We have our own problems, both financial and emotional, to deal with. How much can parents give? We're only human."

Impulsiveness. "We've got to stop our daughter from destroying herself, and we've got to do it now. We don't have time to plan; we're going to grab her out of that situation."

Conflict. "We want to help our daughter, but she's an adult and we feel like intruders trying to step in and help. On the other hand, she is our daughter, and we feel responsible for her well-being. So we're left feeling pulled in opposite directions, and we don't know which way to go."

"Spooky" apprehensions. "I know something is wrong, but I can't quite put my finger on what it is. It's an eerie feeling, reminiscent of horror movies I've seen where people get possessed by spirits and their entire personality changes."

Helplessness, incompetence. "The more I try to reach out and help, the less confident I feel. My words come out clumsy and awkward, and its seems as though I'm always doing the wrong thing."

Rejection, hurt. "I feel that my son's radical change in behavior is his way of pushing me away."

Alarm. "I ran into my son while he was selling flowers in a restaurant and I really panicked. I couldn't think straight, I couldn't hear what he was saying, and I couldn't think of anything to say. I just jumped up from the table and fled. I was totally out of control. And even now, I can't calm down. Every moment I'm thinking about all the terrible things that are probably happening to him."

Although the above thoughts and feelings are both natural and understandable, they may prove debilitating to parents trying to help a child. In counseling parents, we have found that identifying, expressing, and rationally discussing thoughts and feelings allow parents to step back and assess their situations from a broader, calmer perspective.

Mr. and Mrs. Rose, for example, were so alarmed about their daughter's intended move into a religious commune that they came to us with a single demand: "Keep her out of there! Don't let her join that group! We don't care how you do it, just make sure that it's done!" After talking about their feelings, which included a fear for their daughter's well-being and a lack of confidence in their own ability to help, the Roses felt less urgent, less driven. They decided to spend some time evaluating their situation before taking any steps towards intervention.

In another case, Mr. and Mrs. Brown blamed each other for their son Jimmy's abrupt decision to leave college and become a full-time cult recruiter. Mr. Brown accused his wife of "pressuring Jimmy to finish college when what he really needed was time to think about a career." Mrs. Brown accused her husband of "pampering Jimmy to the point where he felt no sense of responsibility to become an independent adult." In our counseling sessions, talking about their feelings helped them realize that although each of them may have contributed to Jimmy's decision, blaming each other was not an effective means of helping their son.

Common Parental Reactions to Behavioral Changes

Once they perceive a behavioral change in their child, parents may respond in a number of ways.

Below we identify and briefly assess some of the more commonly reported reactions of parents to disturbing behavior changes in their child.

Unaware
The unaware parent doesn't recognize significant behavior changes in a child. This may be due to limited contact. For example, when Mona went away to college her parents weren't aware of any problems until they started receiving distress signals in Mona's letters. Or, the child may be effectively deceptive, for example, acting normally around his parents but behaving uncharacteristically whenever he's out of their range. Or, the parents may be going through a crisis or major life transition which impedes their capacity to notice changes in their child.

Approve
The approving parent perceives the child's behavior change as positive, as in the following examples:

- The Woods were at one point relieved that Mona had joined a "wonderful group of young people interested in the Bible with whom she felt comfortable."
- A mother is "glad my daughter became a vegetarian. I've read that it's healthier, and I have even considered giving up meat myself."
- "It's about time my son straightened out. His short hair and neat appearance are a welcome relief. I was worried he'd be a hippie forever."
- "My son has a new group of friends. They must be extremely intelligent, because suddenly he sounds like an expert on psychology. I'm very proud."
- "My daughter does meditation and it really seems to calm her down."

Becoming a vegetarian, "straightening out," converting to a new religion, using a new vocabulary, and many other changes may be positive for certain individuals. On the other hand, changes which are perceived as beneficial by parents may in fact be harmful. For example, becoming a vegetarian may reflect a child's unquestioning adherence to a cult doctrine. Often, the harm or benefit of a behavior change can only be determined after the cause and context of the change is known.

Deny or Diminish the Importance of the Change

When confronted with objective evidence that a child's behavior has changed radically, some parents react by denying or diminishing the significance of the change. For example, a close friend informs a parent, "Your son told me he is in the Moonies. You know, that's a destructive cult." The parent who reacts with denial might say, "Oh no, you must be mistaken. My son would never get involved in something like that." The parent who diminishes the importance might say, "So what? He still calls home."

Avoiding

These parents are aware of a change and may feel that something is wrong, but choose not to address the problem directly. For example:

- "At the time our son moved into a commune, we were dealing with the death of our youngest child. Although his move troubled us, we decided not to make an issue out of it, and never spoke to him about it."
- "I felt so guilty when my daughter told me about her plans to get divorced that I couldn't face her. I just kept thinking it was my fault, because her father and I were divorced a few years ago."
- "When our daughter dropped out of college, we didn't voice our objections because we were afraid she would get upset."

Disapproving

Parents may respond by disapproving of the behavior change itself or by disapproving of the child. For example, a son in college starts practicing an Eastern meditation.

Disapprove of behavior. "I'm troubled by the effects this meditation seems to have on you. You're more withdrawn, less responsive to us and to your friends. You seem to have lost interest in the pleasures of life, you gave up pursuing your career, and now you've given away nearly all of your possessions. We are worried about the way you're acting." (*Note:* These comments communicate how the parents feel about specific behavior. They are "I" statements, and are not accusatory.)

Disapprove of child. "You're rebelling against us. Why don't you grow up? This Eastern garbage is against our religion. You're really slapping us in the face. You're destroying our marriage. Why can't you ever do anything normal?" (*Note:* These comments, though they may be spoken with sincere concern, are accusatory and communicate disrespect for a child's integrity and ideals.)

Passive Concern
These parents acknowledge that something is wrong and believe that the best response is non-intervention. They may feel their child is just going through a phase and will eventually resume normal activities, or they may think they don't have the right to impose on the privacy and autonomy of their adult child.

Active Concern
Parents responding with active concern might say, "Something is definitely wrong with our child, and we must do something to help." This reaction may take time to emerge. Days, weeks, months, even years may pass while parents witness isolated incidents of incongruous behavior without recognizing that there is a significant problem. Suddenly, a conversation, an argument, a telephone call, a letter, a newspaper article, a comment from a friend, or some other relatively minor stimulus brings everything into sharp focus and the parent realizes that something is wrong and "I've got to try to help my child." The following case illustrates such a progression of awareness:

Jerry began spending a lot of his time with a self-awareness therapy group. For the first six months his parents were unaware of his involvement. He lived in California and they resided in Maine, and although they spoke weekly by telephone there were many details in Jerry's life about which they knew very little.

Jerry's commitment to the group started interfering with his marriage when he tried to recruit his wife. Her refusal to join became a sore spot in their relationship. Jerry's parents were aware of the conflict but thought, "Right now he's really excited about the group because it's a new experience. When the initial high wears off he'll stop pestering his wife."

But unfortunately they were mistaken. The marriage started deteriorating rapidly, and within a year of joining the group Jerry insisted on getting a divorce. Initially his parents avoided commenting because "We didn't want to incur Jerry's wrath. He would get so defensive whenever we tried to discuss the matter with him." But their laissez-faire stance gave way to overt disapproval when Jerry quit his job and refused to pay child support. They chided him, "Jerry, you're being irresponsible. Instead of quitting your job you should have left that therapy group and returned home to your wife and child. Why don't you grow up?" But disapproval did not make Jerry change his mind, and they resigned themselves to waiting it out: "He'll see his mistake eventually. It's only a matter of time."

But five years later, his marriage over, Jerry was devoting himself full time to recruiting new members for the therapy group. He seemed a changed person. It all became painfully clear when Jerry's youngest brother, Ethan, was killed in a car accident and Jerry refused to come home for the funeral. He excused himself, saying, "Each of us creates his own world. Ethan must have wanted to die. There's no need for me to come home." At that point his parents realized, "Something is wrong with our child, and we must do something to help."

The Woods also went through a process that began with a lack of awareness but gradually developed into an active concern for Mona. As with many parents, they chided themselves for being too slow in recognizing that Mona was in a dangerous situation. But no one is capable of predicting the future, and Mona's initial loneliness at college might have developed into something positive had she not been recruited by a cult. Thus the Woods cannot be blamed for this sorry twist of fate. Had they jumped in to rescue Mona from every discomfort, they might have stifled much of her growth.

Truly, there is no advantage to self-flagellation over past reactions, since none of those can be changed. It is possible, however, for parents to identify and understand their behavior, and to develop more constructive ways of responding in the future.

Chapter Four

Problem-Solving: Preparing Yourself

The following pages present a model for problem-solving which is designed for parents whose son or daughter has undergone a disturbing change in personality and behavior and who suspect their child is in a destructive cult. On a practical level, we offer suggestions to help parents develop a constructive attitude, learn basic skills, and choose an appropriate strategy to help their child. Our more general and long-range goals are (1) to help promote a child's autonomy and freedom to develop his or her potential, and (2) to help parents maintain or develop a healthy parent-child relationship.

We stress from the start that *there is no set pattern or formula that can guarantee success*. Parents must extract from these pages that which is relevant and useful in light of their particular situation, their capabilities and limitations, and the particular needs, concerns, and capabilities of their son or daughter.

In addition to reading this manual, we encourage parents to employ creativity and common sense, to consult other information sources (some of which are noted here), and to seek dependable outside support.

Three Problem-Solving Approaches

Below we examine three ways of addressing a problem. The first two, "Taking Over" and "Laissez-Faire," are common parental approaches to a child in a cult. The third, "Learner-Helper," is the approach we suggest and try to teach to parents who seek us out for counseling.

Taking Over
Using this approach, parents who perceive a problem with their son or daughter try to assume control of the situation and rectify the problem themselves. For example, John, 23, graduates from college and moves into a small commune in Idaho. His parents, who live in Florida, don't know anything about the commune, but they are aware of cults and are afraid that John has become part of such a group. Perceiving the situation as "very dangerous," they fly across the country, plop themselves on his doorstep, and proclaim, "We're not leaving until you move out of here!"

There are a number of reasons why parents may employ the "Taking Over" approach: the desire for quick relief from stress, the desire to gain control over an uncomfortable situation or an "unruly" child, or the instinct to save a child who appears to be in imminent danger.

Indeed, when a child's physical or psychological well-being is threatened, taking over may be appropriate, and may in fact be the only means of helping him. On the other hand, when a situation is not life-threatening, there are a number of risks involved which parents should consider before they act. First, an adult child may construe this approach to be an extreme and unnecessary violation of his privacy and autonomy, and a blatant attack on his integrity and ideals. At worst, he may become so angry that he cuts off all communication with his parents, making future attempts at helping much more difficult.

A second risk is that their own sense of urgency may lead parents to make rash, unwise decisions. For example, they may misdiagnose the problem; or, they may enlist the aid of an irresponsible "expert" who does more harm than good; or they may exhaust their financial, emotional, and other resources prematurely.

Because of these risks, parents who think they should take over might first ask themselves:

- "Is my child really in need of immediate rescue? Is there time to assess the situation more thoroughly before deciding on a course of action?"
- "What is motivating me to take over? Is it a reasoned reaction to danger? Or am I impatient, frustrated, angry, etc.?"
- "By taking over, am I keeping my child's best interests in mind?"

Laissez-Faire
(*Note:* This approach is similar to the passive concern reaction described in Chapter Three, *The Parents' Experience*).

Once a son or daughter has reached a certain age, be it 16, 18, 21, or 30, many parents feel that the time has arrived for the child to bear the consequences of his or her mistakes. "How else," they ask, "will my child learn to accept adult responsibilities?"

It is hard to dispute the idea that adults should be accountable for their actions. But what happens when a 34-year-old daughter gets caught in a harmful situation from which she can't extricate herself? Where should parents draw the line between letting their child make and learn from her own mistakes, on the one hand, and fulfilling parental obligations to protect her from harm, on the other? Is there any way to respect a child's integrity and autonomy and still help her?

These questions, while difficult to answer, lead us into an exploration of the Learner-Helper Approach.

Learner-Helper

Let's consider the example of a 21-year-old woman who drops out of college to become a religious missionary. Parents taking the learner-helper approach might say, "We think our daughter is in trouble. We want to help her, if that's what's best for her. But first we need information, we need to learn, and we are willing to change our own views and behavior, if necessary, so that we can help. Whatever actions we take, we want to respect our child's integrity, autonomy, privacy, and ideals. We want to be as flexible and unimposing as possible." In essence, these parents want to help their daughter help herself.

On the negative side, the learner-helper approach is time-consuming and emotionally trying. It often demands a change in parents' goals, expectations, and ways of communicating, and may require putting one's own feelings, activities, interests, and plans on hold. It is a long-term investment in the personal well-being of the child and in the parent-child relationship. There is often no immediate relief from stress. There are no guarantees that this investment will prove fruitful, although the same is true of any approach. There are no pat formulas, only a variety of suggestions which may or may not pertain to a particular situation. And finally, this approach may not be feasible for parents who have no contact, or very limited contact, with their child.

Turning now to the benefits — it has been our experience, as clinicians, that parents who adopt the learner-helper approach are more likely to obtain information, learn skills, and cultivate attitudes that make them more effective problem-solvers, better able to help their sons and daughters. In addition, we favor this approach because:

- it is open-ended and flexible, with room for changing goals and strategies;
- it is based on information, reasoning, and intuition;
- it respects the autonomy, integrity, intelligence and concerns of both the child and the parents;
- it promotes a constructive, satisfying parent-child relationship.

Preparation for Problem-Solving

It is not enough to plant the seed. One must first prepare the soil.

There are a number of things parents can do to help set up a supportive climate for problem-solving. Below, we outline some practical first steps — often simultaneous or overlapping — in problem-solving preparation.

Step Back

Disturbing thoughts and feelings such as alarm, dismay, despair, panic, guilt and rage are obstacles to clear, informed decision-making. In counseling parents, we try to help them overcome these obstacles so they can approach the problem with a clear mind. The following are some suggestions for stepping back:

Assess your personal strengths. Remember, you have solved problems before. Think of times when you have dealt successfully with problems. Ask yourself, "What personal qualities helped me in these situations (for example, persistence, patience, confidence, sense of humor, being organized)?" Make a list of your personal strengths.

Assess your resources.
- **Time.** How much time do you have to address this problem? Can your schedule be adjusted if necessary?
- **Money.** Are there financial resources you can draw upon should the need arise for such things as counseling, travel, informational materials, etc.?
- **Emotional support.** One of the most valuable assets in problem-solving is a friend from whom you can get both an honest second opinion and emotional support. In some families, spouses prefer to turn to each other, exclusively, for second opinions. Other parents find comfort in having someone outside the family as a confidant. While it is important for parents to do what is most comfortable for them, we do encourage parents to seek an outside opinion and source of emotional support (that is, in addition to spouses supporting each other). However, we advise parents to exercise care in choosing the person or persons with whom they will discuss the problem, and we offer the following questions to help make this choice:

  - Which persons have the time to address the problem carefully? Are they trustworthy, reliable, and able to maintain confidentiality?
  - Are there professionals (counselors, clergy, social workers, teachers, etc.), relatives, or friends, who might have pertinent information and experience?
  - Who will listen carefully and respond honestly?
  - Which persons seem to have a good relationship with your child? Know what's going on in your child's life?
  - Which persons are listeners rather than advice givers?

Acknowledge your limitations. Try to confine your involvement to that which is reasonable, possible, and healthy in light of your current circumstances.

Set reasonable priorities. If your first concern is to help your child, be aware that some of your own needs may have to go unmet until a later date.

As you begin to set priorities, you may discover that there are other problems which take precedence over helping a child, for example: taking care of personal health; fulfilling responsibilities to another child; resolving financial, emotional, or situational stresses. We encourage parents to identify and resolve any immediate issues that might interfere with effective problem-solving at a later date.

In some cases, a parent may decide to wait for a spouse's support. For example, when Mrs. Wood realized that Mona was in a destructive cult and needed help, Mr. Wood was not ready to take action. Mrs. Wood decided that her first priority was to resolve this conflict with her husband, rather than try to help Mona all by herself. (Counseling may be especially helpful in situations in which spouses disagree.)

In some families, parents may be able to start helping their child while attending to their own needs at the same time, that is, they "orchestrate" their priorities.

Cultivate an Effective Problem-Solving Attitude
Attitude is a crucial, though often neglected aspect of problem-solving. Most people in distress ask, "What should I do?," and not, "What should my attitude be?" Below is a list of factors that facilitate problem-solving.

Patience. Not only a virtue, patience is also an asset to the problem-solver. Be patient, first of all, with yourself. Try not to limit yourself to a predetermined time schedule. Don't expect to perform miracles, and try not to expect others whose support you enlist to know everything or to "make everything all right." (Families with a child in danger will of course have much less time to make decisions. But a sense of urgency should not become an excuse for impatience.) Above all, try to be patient with your child. If it becomes clear that your son or daughter is in a destructive cult, it is important to remember that cult involvement can have profound effects on members. It sometimes takes years for a former member to firmly reestablish herself in the non-cult world. Pushing unrealistically for a quick resolution often makes things worse.

Willingness to learn.
- to gather and assimilate information from a variety of sources;
- to welcome new, conflicting, and diverse ideas;
- to brainstorm with and respect the opinions of others;
- to withhold criticism and judgment, and delay decision-making until adequate information has been obtained
- to admit error or defeat, when appropriate.

Willingness to change. Creatures of habit, human beings do not take easily to change. But this is an essential element of problem-solving. Dealing with a possible cult involvement may require parents to make the following changes.

- **Change your perception of the problem:** As you gather new information and think about the problem, you may need to adjust your perceptions. Thus, parents who initially think their child is in a destructive cult may discover that the group is not harmful. In this case, if the child's behavior seems odd or disturbing, something else may be wrong. (See Chapter Six: Defining the Problem). Or, upon investigating a child's behavior, parents may discover that there is no problem at all. Or, there may be multiple problems, such as, a destructive cult involvement and serious psychological problems as well. Parents should allow for all possibilities.

- **Change your expectations:** Parents may need to modify their expectations so that they are more realistic and in line with the wishes and capabilities of their child. This can be very disappointing, especially when a son or daughter is not endowed with capabilities and interests that the parents had hoped for. In order to help, therefore, parents must tailor their efforts towards the real child, and not towards some hoped-for ideal.

- **Change your priorities:** for example, attending to a child's ill health may take priority over trying to get her to leave a destructive cult. Or, the time required for problem-solving, no matter how well planned, may unexpectedly interfere with a parent's vocational aspirations or commitments (for example, making it impossible for a parent to attend an important business conference). Anticipating that there may be conflicts over priorities may lessen the anxiety, should the time come to make one of these difficult choices.

- **Change your behavior patterns:** Problem-solving demands a willingness to trade old, familiar behavior patterns for new ones. For example, parents who have always assumed an authoritarian posture with their child may find that this type of relationship impedes communication. (A more detailed discussion of parent-child communication can be found in Chapter Eight).

Take Care of Yourself
Try to maintain good physical and psychological health. Be careful not to exhaust yourself or your resources; find sources of replenishment such as exercise, emotional release, pleasurable distractions. Seek help (professional and/or non-professional) when you need it.

Be Organized
Keep files and written records of all information, including telephone numbers, names and addresses, useful books, magazines, and newspaper articles, financial transactions, etc., so that you have immediate access to your resources. Also, it is often helpful to save letters and to write down descriptions of significant interactions you have with your child.

- **Organize your time** efficiently.

- **Plan ahead**, trying to leave as little as possible to chance without being rigid or controlling. In one case, for example, a counselor urged a father to try to be passive, because the child interpreted the father's problem-solving attempts as "control," against which the child rebelled by avoiding his parents.

Ongoing Assessment

At least once, and preferably twice a week, set aside time to think about, discuss, and write down your thoughts about the situation, asking such questions as:

- How are my resources (physical, emotional, financial) holding out?
- Do I need to rearrange my priorities? In what ways?
- Has my attitude been constructive? Has my behavior been effective? If not, can I change these for the better?
- Am I taking care of myself?
- Do I need help? In what areas?

Chapter Five

Defining the Problem

Just as a good physician doesn't dispense drugs carelessly, we withhold prescriptions or suggestions for intervention until parents have clearly identified both the symptoms (that is, the particular disturbing behavior) and the causes of their child's problem.

In our counseling sessions, parents have found that their initial impressions are not always accurate. Sometimes a seemingly serious problem, under inspection, turns out to be a minor misunderstanding. In other cases, parents discover that the roots of their child's disturbing behavior are much more complex than at first appeared. For this reason, we strongly advise parents to be "scientists" and to sort and test their perceptions of the problem before taking any remedial action.

This chapter is designed as an aid in testing perceptions. The first part deals with identifying and evaluating symptoms — What are they? Why are they troubling?

The second and third parts of the chapter are concerned with identifying the causes of the problem. In the second part we introduce a number of non-cult factors that may have contributed to or caused a child's disturbing behavior; the third part aims to help parents determine whether a child is in a destructive cult.

Examining the Symptoms

As you begin to identify and evaluate your child's symptoms, it may help to review Chapter Four, "The Parents' Experience," where we cite examples of behavior that cause parents to worry. Since our list is by no means exhaustive, you may find that other behavior has prompted your concern. Also, as you reflect upon the following questions, we suggest writing down your responses. This will save you the trouble of having to recall the same information over and over again in your mind, since this information may come in handy at various points in the problem-solving process.

If your child belongs to a dubious group, pretend he wasn't in such a group and ask yourself if any of his specific behavior would trouble you.

- *What specific behavior do you find disturbing?* Secrecy? Uncharacteristic vocabulary or speech patterns? Emotional changes? Shift in friends and activities? Disturbing sexual attitudes? Rejection of secular goals? Dubious financial activities? Abrupt marital decision? Shifts in religious, philosophical, or political views? Extreme commitments? Unconventional lifestyle? Change in appearance? Vocational turnabout? Indication of psychological distress? Diminished academic performance? Other behavior you find disturbing?

- *Why is this behavior troubling?* Are you disappointed because your son or daughter hasn't met your expectations? Do you feel rejected? Embarrassed or ashamed? Does your child appear to be in danger of physical or psychological harm? Are there other concerns causing you to worry?
- *Do you need more information before you can evaluate your child's symptoms?* What types of information do you need? What information is most important to your immediate action needs? How can you obtain this information?
- *What do you perceive to be the causes of the behavior?* Cultic manipulation? Psychological problems? Family conflicts? Situational stresses?

Possible Non-Cult Causes (or Contributory Causes) of Disturbing Behavior Change

Inexplicable shifts in a child's behavior can be very disconcerting to parents. Not knowing why a child has changed makes it very difficult to evaluate the situation and respond effectively. In the following pages we explore some non-cult factors that may contribute to or cause disturbing changes in a child's behavior.

Why explore non-cult factors? When parents seek our counsel they are often quite sure that their son or daughter is in a cult. Many of them are initially perplexed, even reluctant, when asked to consider non-cult factors. However, in more cases than not, there are both cult and non-cult factors influencing their child. And in some cases, cult factors simply aren't present. Recognizing these factors has proven helpful in assessing and responding to a child's behavior change.

Normal Adolescent Challenges

Adolescents and young adults face many challenges which are a normal part of growing up. Choices have to be made about schooling and career, sexuality and marriage, lifestyle and values. In addition, the challenge to become autonomous, financially and emotionally independent of one's parents, is keenly felt at this age.

In meeting these challenges, teenagers and young adults may try out a variety of lifestyles, values, and activities which — although not inherently harmful — may be disturbing or even alarming to parents. For example:

- The son of a successful businessman chooses an academic career in 19th century English literature, a field which seems highly impractical to his parents.

- A senior in high school decides not to go to college, despite the fact that her parents place a high value on education. She is not interested in academics right now, and has a strong desire to earn money and take on the responsibility of a full-time job.
- A teenager refuses to participate in social activities with his parents, preferring to spend time alone or with his peers.
- A young woman who never questioned her parents' belief that "abortion is wrong" becomes an ardent pro-choice advocate.
- The teenager whose parents are politically liberal decides to support a conservative candidate for president.
- The son of non-religious parents becomes active in the family's religion or in some other religious group.
- The daughter of wealthy parents decides to live very modestly and donate most of her money to charity.

Although these situations may be frustrating or disappointing for parents, they may in fact be signals that a child is growing up — making and taking responsibility for adult decisions. On the other hand, they may indicate a problem, either with the child, with the parents, or between the child and parents.

Parents who feel something is wrong with their child might first try to determine whether the behavior is actually harmful, or whether perhaps their concern stems from the disappointment of watching their child grow up in a manner different from their own hopes and expectations. The following questions may be helpful: Which behavior is upsetting? In what ways, if any, is my child being harmed? If I can't think of any specific harms, why am I upset? Do I have ambivalent feelings about my child growing up? Do I feel threatened or alienated by his different lifestyle and values? Am I angry or disappointed because she didn't choose the career I had in mind for her? Do I feel rejected because he no longer relies on me for emotional support or to answer his questions about life? Are my expectations realistic and healthy? Are my goals aligned with my daughter's goals and abilities?

Answering these questions may help pinpoint the thoughts, feelings, and behavior which are provoking anxiety. If parents determine that the "problem" seems to be their own adjustment to a child growing up, it really should be the parents, and not the child, who try to adapt to the changes. They can make an effort to acknowledge the child's need to break away. They can learn to view differences in style, values, and opinions as a sign of their child's growing autonomy and independence, rather than as an intentional blow against them. They can allow their child to make her own mistakes and bear the consequences. Although parents' greater wisdom may enable them to see the danger inherent in certain of their child's autonomous decisions, parents must, if they are to respect that autonomy, focus on giving advice rather than "orders."

If a child does seem to be having trouble meeting developmental challenges, parents might consider discussing their thoughts with each other, with a counselor, and/or with their child.

Talking things over with a teenager or young adult may not be an easy task. Many are hesitant to discuss personal matters with their parents. Also, parents often feel awkward discussing certain issues, for example, sexuality, with their children. On the other hand, if parents exhibit interest and openness, and try to initiate discussions that aren't threatening or judgmental, they may discover that their teenager is eager to talk with a trustworthy and loving parent.

In later chapters, parent-child communication is addressed in greater detail.

In sum, developmental challenges may prompt teenagers and young adults to act in ways that alarm parents, but these actions need not necessarily indicate that the child is in trouble. To accurately "diagnose" the situation, parents are advised to examine their own thoughts and feelings, try to discuss their concerns — if possible — with their son or daughter, and attempt to understand the cause of the upsetting behavior.

Situational Stress
The following are just a few examples of situations that often provoke uncharacteristic, disturbing behavior:

- An adolescent may react to the *untimely death* of a parent, sibling, or friend by temporarily withdrawing from his family and friends.
- Sudden *financial hardship* may evoke childish behavior in a young adult who is aspiring towards independence.
- A teenager experiencing *work-related problems* may suddenly become belligerent towards her parents.
- A *deteriorating marriage or intimate relationship* may result in a spurt of blatant promiscuity or a disinterest in finding a partner.
- *Academic stresses* may give rise to thoughts of suicide or result in other self-destructive behavior (for example, immoderate drinking, drug abuse, overeating, etc.)

Quite often, the alarming behavior that results from situational stresses is just a temporary reaction that subsides with the passing of time, as often happens after a period of mourning or grief. However, if the behavior persists, or seems imminently dangerous, parents might well consider offering help, or, if they desire assistance, obtaining professional guidance.

Psychiatric or psychological disorders may be at the root of such behavior changes as wild mood swings, paranoid thoughts, distorted perceptions of reality, absence of all emotion, incoherent speech, prolonged depression, or severe restlessness. If parents suspect that a child's behavior changes are due to mental distress, they may want to consult a mental health professional, or tactfully suggest to their child that he seek professional assistance. Some psychiatric disorders, such as certain types of depression, have significant biological components; laymen can waste much time seeking to change biologically-rooted disturbing behavior through just talking and encouragement.

Physical disorders such as mononucleosis, hypoglycemia, thyroid dysfunctions, and diabetes, to name just a few, are often accompanied by pronounced changes in behavior. If this is a possibility, parents should seek the advice of a physician.

Substance abuse, that is, excessive use of drugs (prescription or non-prescription) or alcohol, may be responsible for such behavior as excessive secrecy, incoherent speech, poor concentration, giddiness, mood swings, irresponsibility, clumsiness, emotional withdrawal, and failure in school. Parents who suspect this is a factor influencing their child's behavior should seek information and support from organizations that specialize in serving those with substance abuse problems. Here, too, physicians and social service agencies should be consulted for reliable, competent references.

Religious Conversion

For some people, religious conversion is a subtle, evolving, and essentially formal confirmation or acceptance of personal religious views. A second type of religious conversion is marked by radical changes in world-view, beliefs, and values, as well as a sudden enthusiasm for activities that center on religious aims and ideas. Recent converts may talk excitedly, even effusively, about new feelings of a higher purpose in life, spiritual renewal, ecstasy, a sudden awareness of God, and confidence that they have been "saved." In our discussion of religious conversion, below, we are referring to this second, more radical conversion process, not characterized by the manipulation of outside forces, as is often the case in cultic conversions.

In some cases, conversion experiences may effect positive changes. For example, people who were previously distressed may feel a new sense of purpose, productiveness, enthusiasm, and liberation, which enables them to live better integrated and more meaningful lives.

Even in the face of positive changes, though, parents may become alarmed. First, because the early stages of many conversions are marked by turmoil and melancholy. Second, drastic changes, whether good or bad, can be frightening, because they are not easily explained or understood. Third, the changes may conflict with parents' values, as when the son of non-religious parents enters a monastery. And finally, conversion to destructive cults may evoke similar symptoms, and parents who are aware of these groups may feel alarmed even if their child has converted to a benign group or traditional religion.

A frequent dilemma for parents, then, is how to distinguish between harmful and adaptive conversions. Below we give a simplified comparison of the two types.

Adaptive conversion.

- The convert is motivated primarily by internally generated searching.
- The new belief system is at least relatively open and tolerant of other views.
- The convert's critical faculties remain intact or are enhanced.
- The convert's autonomy remains intact or is enhanced.
- The convert is well integrated, in that various aspects of his life (values, social relationships, personal history, talents, goals, educational achievements, and the like) are coherently incorporated into the new outlook and behavior.

Harmful conversion.

- This type of conversion is provoked by manipulation and pressure from outside forces (for example, the group).
- The new belief system is simplistic, absolutist, and intolerant of other views.
- Critical thinking is denigrated, and the convert's critical abilities are impaired.
- The convert's autonomy is diminished.
- The convert is poorly integrated, that is, has undergone a radical personality change in which parts of the self are rigidly compartmentalized, has severed ties with past friends and family, denies or diminishes the importance of personal history.
- The convert is exploited financially and/or psychologically by a group.

Note: *The Varieties of Religious Experience*, by William James, offers a much more comprehensive description of sudden religious conversion. Also, Part III of this chapter may help parents determine whether a child's conversion is adaptive or harmful.

Problems Within the Family

Family problems often affect a child. They may contribute to or cause a child's disturbing behavior. They may influence (and often reduce) parents' effectiveness in helping a son or daughter. And they may require immediate attention.

As mental health professionals, we encourage parents to identify family problems, and offer the following questions for consideration. If, after reflecting on these, you recognize significant family problems that require attention, you might consider open family discussion, family counseling, or individual counseling as a prerequisite to helping your child.

As you consider each question, ask yourself:

(1) Might these problems be affecting your child? How?
(2) Might they interfere with efforts to help? How?

(3) Should they be given attention *before* you try to help?

- Are there medical problems within your family?
- Are there marital conflicts?
- Are there financial problems? Business or career difficulties? Unemployment?
- Are there psychiatric or psychological problems in the family? Hospitalizations? Suicide attempts?
- Are there religious conflicts within the family? Intermarriage? Ambivalence regarding religious practice, education, values, beliefs? Anti-religious sentiments? Absence of religious affiliation? Is there an inordinate pressure to conform to particular religious practices or beliefs?
- Are there family communication problems? Frequent arguments? Anger, hostility, frustration? Emotional distance? Lack of information-sharing? Little or no contact among members? Indifference?
- Is there physical/sexual abuse in the family?
- Are there problems with siblings, grandparents, other blood relatives?
- What are your family's major strengths? How can these assets be mobilized to assist in problem solving?
- What are your family's major weaknesses? How can they be prevented from interfering with problem solving?
- How does your family, as a group, cope with stress? What are your strong points? Weak points?
- Are there other family problems that might be contributing to or causing your child's disturbing behavior? OR, other problems that might interfere with efforts to help? OR, other problems requiring immediate attention?

Is Your Son's or Daughter's Disturbing Behavior the Result of Involvement in a Destructive Cult? Questions and Possible Answers

Is Your Son or Daughter Involved with a Group? If not, then the behavior changes you have observed may be the result of other factors.

If yes, then...

Is the Group Destructive?

Informational resources. To determine whether or not a group is destructive, it is important to become knowledgeable about cults and the particular group with which your child is affiliated. Chapter Three gives a very general overview of cults, and needs supplementing. Further information can be obtained through the readings listed in the Appendix.

It can also be helpful to study literature of the group with which your child is involved. Reading this will help familiarize parents with the group's language, philosophy, beliefs, practices, and activities, and may help parents communicate more effectively with their child. Destructive cults, however, often have two sets of literature: one, for public consumption; the other, for members only. Often, the public literature falls far short of providing an honest, accurate picture of the group.

Much knowledge can be gained by visiting the group or attending its public meetings. Visiting provides first-hand information about the group's beliefs, practices, lifestyle, and members. Within the group context, parents can better evaluate the nature and degree of their son's or daughter's involvement.

Attending an introductory meeting or other group activity at a child's request, while providing further information, may also enhance parent-child relations by making the child feel that her parents respect her interests and ideals. (For example, Mona was reassured by her parents' attendance at her cult college graduation and, therefore, felt safe enough to visit her parents for the weekend without being accompanied by another member of the fellowship.) Finally, attending a group activity gives parents a shared experience which they can discuss with their son or daughter afterwards.

Note of Caution: Before visiting the group or attending a meeting, parents should wait, if at all possible, until they have at least some general knowledge about the group. There are some very sad accounts of people who attended one cult meeting — "just to find out" — and never returned. Others have been manipulated into believing that the group is "okay" when in fact it is highly exploitative. Successful con men seem like "nice guys," or they wouldn't be successful.

Checklist. After you gather general information on cults and specific information about your child's group, you can begin to answer the question, "Is the group destructive?" Below is a checklist of items to consider in your evaluation. Note that these are merely criteria to weigh. Not all need be present to deem a group destructive, nor is there a definite boundary between destructive and benign.

- *What are the recruitment techniques?* Are they manipulative? Deceptive? In what ways?
- *What promises are made?* Are they realistic? Are they honored?
- *Are the beliefs regarded as absolute, ultimate truth, and above secular law?*
- *What is the attitude toward the leader?* Is the leader's photograph displayed excessively? Are members taught to be subservient, passive, obedient, or blindly faithful?
- *What is the view toward the non-cult world?* Benevolent? Paranoid? Neutral? Hostile? Evil? Impure? An illusion? Materialistic? Satanic?
- *How does the group look upon individuality?* Is it encouraged, discouraged, suppressed? Are the group goals more important than individual goals? Do group needs supersede those of the individual members? If you have met

several members, is there a distinct personality shared by all or many of the members?

- *Are there prescriptions for a particular lifestyle, dress, diet, sexual practices?* Are these rules unduly restrictive? Licentious? Healthy? Unhealthy? Neutral? Benign? In what ways?
- *Do members practice trance-induction techniques such as:* Meditation, chanting, speaking in tongues, etc.? How frequently? Toward what ends? For relaxation? For suppressing doubts?
- *Do members have access to outside information?* What is the group's attitude toward television, newspapers, radio, outside opinions?
- *How does the group look upon traditional religion?* With respect? Contempt? Indifference?
- *Does the group value, encourage, or discourage members from pursuing secular education?* Associating with family? With friends?
- *Does the group respect members' privacy?* Their autonomy?
- *Is there an exclusive language or jargon?* Are ordinary words ascribed new meanings? Are many words and phrases borrowed from foreign languages?
- *Are there secret initiation rites?* Other secret rituals?
- *What is the group's attitude toward the mind?* Is rational thinking denigrated? Encouraged? Are feelings valued over thoughts? Is criticism of the group encouraged? Tolerated? Suppressed?
- *What is the group's attitude toward a member's past* interests, relationships, family? Welcoming? Tolerant? Indifferent? Contemptuous?
- *Are there consequences attached to leaving?* What are they?
- *Does the group adhere to the philosophy that the ends justify the means?* If so, to what extent?
- *Are there financial obligations for members?* What are they? Are they extreme? Implicit? Explicit? Are members left without financial resources of their own? Where does the money go?
- *What is the leader's lifestyle?* Extravagant? Humble? Is the leader accessible, or surrounded by security guards? Does he (or she) practice what he preaches? Is there a discrepancy between the lifestyle of members and that of the leader? Is the leader regarded as teacher? Parent? Lover? Therapist? Magician? God?
- *Is there ongoing indoctrination?* Daily? Weekly? Monthly? What type of indoctrination? Group sessions? Tapes? One-to-one conversations? Reading cult literature? Are questioning and disagreement permitted?
- *At meetings, or among themselves, are new members pressured to reveal extremely personal, self-incriminating information?*

The above checklist is a guide for gathering and evaluating information about the group to which your child belongs. If, after careful consideration, parents determine that the group is **not** destructive, then a child's disturbing behavior may be rooted in other factors. These parents are advised to review Part II of this chapter, and to reconsider non-cult factors that may be influencing their child. It is possible, for example, that a young adult who has just gone through a tremendous situational stress may develop a cult-like "addiction" to a benign group. Group affiliation may be a temporary crutch to help him cope with life problems.

If, however, the group does appear to be destructive, then.....

Has your child changed since joining the cult? Are these changes beneficial, neutral, or harmful?

Involvement in a destructive cult is often accompanied by marked behavior and personality changes, some destructive, some just different, others constructive. Below is a checklist to help parents determine what, if any, changes their son or daughter has undergone since becoming involved in the cult, and to help evaluate these changes.

- **Language changes.** Does your son or daughter use new words or jargon, or ascribe new meanings to ordinary words? Use unspontaneous, rote-like language when discussing or defending the cult? Is your child more or less articulate? More or less communicative?
- **Changes in mood.** Is your child more withdrawn, distant or indifferent? Bland? Smug? Passive? Defensive? Overenthusiastic? Secretive? Rigid? *Or*, is your child more open and responsive? (Note: **Your** behavior can affect that of your child, for example, **your** hostility may cause her to become defensive.)
- **Change in maturational level.** Does your child seem more or less mature? In what ways? More or less responsible (for example, financially, ethically, socially, etc.)? Dependent on the group for moral values, emotional support, sense of direction? *Or*, does your child seem more self-directed and self-reliant?
- **Change in self-concept.** Is your child newly self-deprecating? Is there a marked change in personal beliefs, values, attitudes, goals, aspirations, interests? Is your child's identity linked with the cult? Does she seem more or less autonomous? In what ways?
- **Intellectual changes.** Does your child denigrate logic, reason, critical thinking, the "mind?" Does he value "feeling" so much more than thought that his judgment seems impaired? Does she practice trance-induction techniques (such as meditation)? Often? Constantly? Only when under stress? Does your child display an impaired ability to think critically about the cult? About other topics? (Note: This does not necessarily mean does she disagree with you.) Is your child unwilling to discuss and consider alternative viewpoints? *Or*, has your child become more open-minded and intellectually oriented?
- **Social changes.** Has your child turned away from former friends and interests? Does your child's daily life center around group members and activities? Does he express disdain, hostility, suspicion, cynicism, paranoia, or intolerance towards the non-cult world? *Or*, is she more sensitive and responsive to the outside world? Does your child engage in

leisure activities or take vacations? Spend time away from the group? Desire or pursue intimate sexual relationships? With cult members only? Does your child avoid calling, writing, or visiting home?

- **Financial changes.** Has your child turned over financial assets to the cult? Other material assets? Has the group or your child requested or demanded money from family, friends, or strangers?
- **Are there signs of malnourishment?** Has there been excessive weight gain or loss? Is your child exhausted, accident- or disease-prone? Has there been a marked change in appearance?

From the above questions and your own observations, you can start evaluating the extent and nature of your child's cult involvement. In the end, of course, parents must rely on their own values, perceptions, and criteria for physical and psychological well-being in judging whether or not the changes are destructive.

If you determine that your child has undergone disturbing changes in personality and behavior as a result of cult membership, OR, is likely to undergo these changes, then.....

What's a parent to do? In this chapter we have provided guidelines to help parents define the symptoms and cause(s) of their child's behavior. The next chapter will examine strategies for responding to a son or daughter in a cult.

Chapter Six

Defining a Strategy

As parents read through this book, and as they learn more about their child's cult involvement, their attitudes and priorities may change. So may their choice as to how they will respond to their child.

Many of the parents we counsel come to us looking for deprogrammers, but after careful deliberation decide on a voluntary approach instead. Others come with the hope that we can persuade their child to participate in voluntary counseling, and, if this possibility seems remote, end up hiring deprogrammers. Other parents find it useful to employ several strategies simultaneously. Neither the authors nor the American Family Foundation recommends deprogramming.

As we have said before, there is no formula that is suitable for every situation, and we urge parents to consider the following factors when choosing a strategy that best matches their unique situation:

- personality and needs of their daughter or son;
- the nature, degree, and consequences of their child's cult involvement;
- the potential benefits and risks of each strategy;
- parents' own strengths, weaknesses, resources, needs, and goals.

Below we describe five different responses to a child in a cult. The first four illustrate some of the goals and strategies commonly expressed by parents we have counseled. The fifth response, Promoting Voluntary Reevaluation, reflects our own work with cult members and their parents, and will be discussed in greater detail throughout the remainder of this book.

Distance

Distancing, dismissing, or disowning a son or daughter is an extreme measure, usually taken by parents only as a last resort. Such parents might tell their son, "If you continue to affiliate with that cult, we will dismiss you from our lives."

Possible Motivation

- Parents may hope that such an extreme position will shake their child up, awaken him to the severity of the situation, and prompt him to choose his parents over the cult.

- Parents may feel unable to tolerate further contact with their son, because of:
  - exasperation, and/or
  - ill health, and/or
  - marital or family conflicts that have arisen as a result of the child's cult involvement, and/or
  - other stresses that demand full attention.

Potential Benefits

- This strategy necessitates a choice. The child can no longer straddle the line between cult and non-cult existence. He must choose between his parents and the cult. There is at least a possibility that he will choose his parents.
- For parents who feel an emotional need to discontinue their relationship with a cult-involved child, this strategy provides, at least on the surface, the desired relief.

Potential Risks

- If the child has been struggling with conflicting cult and non-cult loyalties, he may view his parents' ultimatum as a solution: now he can sever ties with his parents without feeling guilty, since *they* were the ones who forced him to make a choice.
- If the child later becomes disillusioned with the cult, the lack of a family to turn to may make it more difficult for her to leave the group.
- Verbally disowning a child is one thing; dismissing a son or daughter from one's thoughts, feelings, and memories is another, much more difficult task, and one which is rarely, if ever, fully accomplished by parents.

Approve, Look for the Good, Join the Cult

These parents might tell their daughter, "We're happy about your involvement with this group."

Possible Motivation

- Cult effects may appear or actually be constructive, *or*, the benefits may appear to outweigh the harms. For example:
  - since joining the cult, the child has overcome a serious addiction to drugs or alcohol; *or*
  - the child was recruited while in prison, and the cult provided a source of comfort and character building; *or*
  - the cult's beliefs and practices may appear consonant with the parents' values.
- Parents may want to remain in contact with their child, but in a way that causes the least possible disruption in their own lives, due to:
  - limited resources (time, money); *or*

- ill health; *or*
- other, more urgent priorities.
- Parents may not want to provoke parent-child conflict (See **Avoid** reaction in Chapter Three: The Parents' Experience):
  - because they feel uncomfortable dealing with conflict themselves, or
  - they're afraid such conflict might push the child away.
- Parents may act favorably toward or even join the cult with hopes of gathering accurate, in-depth information.
- Parents may view this strategy as a stepping-stone to improved rapport, and eventually to helping a child leave the cult.

Potential Benefits

- Less apparent stress (see Risks, below) for parents and child.
- More likely that parents and child will maintain contact.
- May promote parent-child trust.
- Acknowledges that the cult experience is not entirely bad.
- Child may reveal more information concerning the cult and her feelings about it, if she believes her parents look upon it favorably.

Potential Risks

- If parents are being dishonest with themselves, with their child, or both, by pretending they approve of the cult when they really feel it is harming their child, then:
  - the child may sense this and become suspicious or withdrawn;
  - the parents may find it very burdensome to maintain this charade over a prolonged period of time.
- Parental approval may reinforce a child's feeling that the cult is good, even if she has doubts of her own. This may make her prospects for leaving the cult even more remote than if the parents had been openly disapproving.
- In looking for the good, parents may overlook the harmful effects of the cult on their child.
- If they join the cult, parents may become swept up in it, lose their critical perspective, and become subject to its potentially harmful effects.

Tolerate But Disapprove

These parents are not prepared to play an active role in helping their child leave the cult, but they do express their concern and disapproval directly. They might tell their son, "We don't like this group you're in, but you are our child and we'll just have to tolerate it."

Possible Motivation

- Parents may take a laissez-faire position toward their child, believing he is responsible for his actions and they should not interfere.

- Parents may view this strategy as an initial step toward more direct intervention.
- Parents hope child will leave on his own.
- Parents may be unable or unwilling to feign approval (which usually isn't constructive anyway) and unable to pursue a more active strategy.

Possible Benefits

- Parental concern and disapproval, especially if communicated with respect, may provoke discussion, disagreements, and internal conflicts that lead a child to question his cult involvement. Such dialogue may also provide parents with insights and information about the cult.
- Parents are being straightforward, which may promote honest parent-child communication.
- By demonstrating tolerance, parents may be able to maintain close contact with their child.
- Parents are letting their child know, directly, that they care, even as they disapprove.
- Parents can request reciprocal disapproving toleration from their child, which may promote his critical thinking and independence.

Possible Risks

- Child may withdraw from parental disapproval.
- Inaction on the part of parents may result in a child's remaining in the cult indefinitely.
- Because this approach demands considerable discipline and can generate much conflict in parents, it can be extremely difficult to pursue indefinitely.

Rescue, Deprogramming

Until recently, a majority of parents who wanted to help their child leave a cult thought that deprogramming was their only recourse. By deprogramming we mean the involuntary detainment of a cult member in a non-cult setting, while providing information and emotional support intended to generate questions, doubts, and critical thinking about the cult, and eventually — if the process is successful — prompt her to leave the group. In our case study, Mona Wood's parents were advised, "Deprogramming is the only way."

Possible Motivation

- Child appears to be in imminent physical or psychological danger.
- Parents fear losing contact, for example, if the child is moving to another country to live with cult members; *or*, may be planning to marry within the cult.
- Parents may feel an urgency within themselves to:
  - relieve stress

- resolve the problem as quickly as possible
- Attempts to get the child to leave the cult voluntarily have failed.

Potential Benefits

- The deprogramming environment ensures isolation from cult influence.
- Deprogramming allows intensive, 24-hour-a-day access to child to provide information, support, and encouragement to reevaluate the cult.
- Deprogramming is often a relatively short process (usually, a matter of days), although planning for the deprogramming and for post-deprogramming support for the child may take months.
- Deprogrammers often assume control over the situation, setting up the physical environment, gathering and presenting relevant information, and engaging the cult member in discussion. Many parents prefer the deprogramming approach because it seems to relieve them of some of the responsibility for helping their child. (Other parents prefer to participate more actively.)
- Deprogramming may be the only means of dealing with a crisis or near-hopeless situation.

Potential Risks

- There is no licensing institution for deprogrammers, and it is hard to find objective criteria by which to judge their competence. Often parents end up choosing a particular deprogrammer on the basis of his or her reputation and the parents' own gut feelings. In making this important choice under stress, parents may be taken advantage of financially, or choose an "expert" who does more harm than good.
- Even modestly priced deprogrammings can be financially prohibitive for many parents (often over $10,000).
- Deprogramming requires secrecy throughout the planning period, and this may promote stress.
- Deprogramming often requires dishonesty toward the child, which may strain the parent-child relationship as well as cause ethical discomfort in the parents.
- If the deprogramming is planned hastily, all efforts may focus on getting the child out of the cult, and post-deprogramming needs may be neglected. Thus, if the child does decide to leave the cult, child and parents often feel lost during this very difficult period of readjustment. In some cases, post-deprogramming stress may even provoke a child into returning to the cult.
- Involuntary deprogramming may be unlawful. If it fails (as when, after an extended period of time, the child remains steadfast in her cult commitment and returns to the cult), parents may face lawsuits filed by the cult or even by their own child. The cult may also: harass parents, neighbors, relatives, friends, and professional associates by, for example, threatening them with physical violence; hide the child so that parents cannot make contact; spread

ugly rumors intended to soil parents' reputations, etc.

- If deprogramming fails, parent-child trust may break down, making future attempts at intervention much more difficult.
- If deprogramming is unsuccessful, the child may retreat deeper into the cult.
- Current evidence suggests that deprogramming succeeds in persuading the person to leave the group 60-75% of the time. However, it is not known what percentage of these people might have been helped to leave the group through voluntary means. Furthermore, the evidence suggests that most cults have high rates of voluntary departures. Nevertheless, each case is different and there is no reliable way of predicting whether or not a particular person will leave voluntarily or through deprogramming.

Promoting Voluntary Reevaluation

Some people leave cults without any prompting from their parents. This may be due to any number of factors, including these:

- a strong romantic attachment to someone outside the cult;
- the cult member may have at least partially retained her critical faculties and become dismayed by hypocrisy, greed, or harmful beliefs and practices;
- medical or other personal needs may have been ignored by the cult;
- the cult may encourage the member to leave because she isn't contributing enough money or recruiting enough members;
- homesick feelings for family and pre-cult friends.

A good number of people, however, need some type of outside stimulation before they will consider leaving a cult. Promoting Voluntary Reevaluation is a non-coercive strategy aimed at motivating a member to critically assess the cult (voluntarily) by stimulating her critical faculties through parent-child communication (and often with counseling support). This strategy requires extensive preparation by parents in gathering information, cultivating a constructive attitude, learning communication skills, making critical assessments about the nature and degree of their child's involvement. To implement this strategy, parents must establish and maintain contact, rapport, and good communication with their child. They need to initiate discussions that will stimulate a child's critical thinking and to provide ongoing emotional support. Finally, parents might do well to seek counseling assistance to supplement their efforts.

Possible Motivation

- Parents want to respect their child's autonomy while still playing an active helping role.

- Since their child doesn't seem to be in imminent danger, parents may want to invest the time and effort necessary to assess and respond to the situation in the most effective way possible.

Potential Benefits

- This strategy allows parents to assume the posture of advocates (rather than adversaries), and thus may help promote a good parent-child relationship.
- As a gradual (rather than sudden) process, this strategy
  - is less traumatic for both child and parents;
  - allows time to gather information, develop constructive attitudes and skills, and make careful, informed choices.
- In its aim to stimulate a child's own critical faculties, this strategy respects and may even strengthen her autonomy.

Potential Risks

- Because this is a long-term strategy, it may require parents to endure the stress of an unresolved conflict over an extended period of time. Also, parents may have to put some of their own needs "on hold" while attending to their child.
- While parents are preparing themselves, their child will most likely remain in the cult and may get more deeply involved.
- When the child is geographically distant, it can be a very difficult course of action to follow.

Note: Although our cult counseling work focuses on promoting voluntary re-evaluation, we do not recommend this approach to all parents. Listed below are the minimum conditions under which this strategy is most appropriate:

- Parents have or can establish contact with their child.
- Parents are willing and able to invest time and energy in this process and are willing to learn (if necessary) new, more effective ways of communicating with their son or daughter.
- Parents accept the possibility that all their effort may not produce the result they seek.
- The cult member is not in imminent danger of physical or psychological harm.

Having presented an overview of five strategies for responding to a child in a cult, we will now use the remaining chapters to offer a more detailed, instructive explanation of Promoting Voluntary Reevaluation.

Chapter Seven

Promoting Voluntary Reevaluation of the Cult

Ethical Considerations

Parents attempting to help their child voluntarily reevaluate his cult involvement face an apparent ethical dilemma. On the one hand, they may condemn the cult for using deceptively manipulative techniques of persuasion and control on members. On the other hand, they may not be able to avoid at least a mild, partial use of such techniques in order to facilitate a voluntary reevaluation of cult involvement.

This dilemma is more apparent than real because the ethical propriety of techniques of persuasion and control depends upon the magnitude of deception and manipulation, the goals of the interaction, and the context in which it takes place. These three factors differ significantly in cultic and parent-child relationships. The parents' goal is to protect and advance their child's well-being; the cult's goal is to fulfill the leader's desires. The parents' manipulations are mild; the cult's are extreme. The parents function within the context of an open society, which encourages autonomy and the free flow of information; the cult is a closed society which fosters dependency and systematically inhibits a free flow of information.

The suggestions made below respect the cult member's autonomy and needs. A sense of manipulativeness may enter the parent-child relationship, but this is usually because an appropriate resolution of the conflict between parent and child demands self-control and deliberation on the parents' part. They may, for example, sometimes find it necessary to have hidden agendas. The level of manipulativeness they may need to employ, however, is relatively low. Furthermore, assuming that their child is the victim of a cultic relationship, a moderate caretaker mode is justified because a) the cultist's autonomy and judgment have been diminished, b) the cultist is harmed by the cultic relationship, and c) a person's family traditionally has more ethical latitude in social influence processes involving him than do persons from outside the family.

In conclusion, if they want to maintain their ethical bearings, parents should continually monitor the propriety of their actions. They should avoid using manipulative techniques of influence in order merely to fulfill their goals or needs. And they should make sure that a caretaker mode of relating is called for before resorting to manipulative methods aimed at fulfilling goals and needs of their child.

Establish Rapport

Personal Contact
This is a prerequisite for promoting voluntary reevaluation. If parents have no contact with a child, their first priority is to locate her. If telephone calls and letters go unanswered, visiting the group may yield some information. Also, if a child has become particularly hostile to her parents, she may respond more kindly to letters, phone calls, or visits from siblings, other relatives, or non-cult friends. Finally, parents may need assistance from organizations, agencies, and individuals experienced in helping families of missing cult members. Some resources to explore are listed in the Appendix.

If parents already have contact, they can work on increasing the frequency and quality of that contact by, for example, encouraging their daughter to visit home, and making an effort to visit her. In essence, the more contact parents have, the greater their opportunities will be to help.

Establish Trust
If a child doesn't trust his parents, then they can't have much constructive influence on him. A key element of trust is good communication — an unobstructed flow of information and feelings between parents and child.

Over the years, families develop habits and patterns of communication which either discourage or promote trust. For example, one parent we counseled told us, "Whenever my husband and I had a problem, we tried to hide it from our son. We didn't want him to worry." This type of well-intentioned protectiveness often promotes a pattern of secrecy whereby the children, once they become adults, are reluctant to confide in their parents. In such a family, trust is not being encouraged. In contrast, parents and children who openly express their feelings and solve problems together are more likely to develop a trusting relationship.

No family is perfect. There are always some communication difficulties that need to be resolved. In non-cult families, grown children and their parents can work together to change faulty communication patterns. But in cases where a son or daughter is in a harmful cult, it is up to the parents to learn skills and to initiate and sustain behavior which will improve parent-child communication and trust.

Cults: What Parents Should Know

Communication Skills: Listening, Responding, and Asking Questions

People often participate in a discussion and feel as though they're being good listeners. But listening is more than simply hearing and responding to someone else's words. Listening is a skill. It requires sensitivity not only to the specific words, but also to the more subtle thoughts, feelings, and implications being expressed.

Good listening promotes good communication and helps establish trust. Parents who do not listen well may unintentionally alienate their child. For example:

A child comes home and is talking to his parents about his cult experience. He says, "In meditation I can hear divine music. It's very beautiful." His mother, who has been "listening," happens to be a biologist, and she interjects, "That's ridiculous. Impossible. It's not divine music, it's your blood rushing through your ears!"

Although the mother is most likely correct, her choice of words and tone may interfere with her communication with her son. Why?

Her son has been describing his experiences, and in such a situation the parents have an opportunity to learn about the cult and, at the same time, to improve their rapport with their son. If, as in our example above, parents insist on championing their own ideas and respond with disbelief or ridicule to their son's experiences, they risk pushing him away. He may decide that he can't trust his parents, and therefore that he'd better not say anything about the cult. *Or*, he might decide to stop visiting home, since the time spent there is so unpleasant. All of these consequences are, ironically, exactly the *opposite* of what his parents had hoped would happen!

An alternate approach to this situation is for parents to listen respectfully, ask questions, and encourage their son to talk about his cult experiences, with hopes that he will feel respected, understood, and desirous of continuing to share his thoughts and feelings with his parents.

Going back to the example about divine music, an alternative response might be, "Oh, what exactly is meditation? How do you do it? What does the music sound like? Why do you call it divine?," or other questions which would provide information while communicating respect and interest in their son's activities. Parents may find that one piece of information leads to another. For example, in the course of asking questions, it may become evident that some of the cult practices are secret, and that members aren't supposed to reveal these to their parents. Thus, parents can ask, "Why is the meditation secret?" In this approach, parents are not telling their son that he is foolish, but instead they are expressing interest and curiosity, thereby opening channels of communication and trust. Of course, in asking such questions, tone of voice is critical.

When it appears that a good rapport has been established, in that the child volunteers both information and personal feelings about the cult, parents can *then* begin to ask questions which are non-threatening but which may generate some critical thinking about the cult. For example, "How do you know it's divine music? Have you considered that it might be something else?" Here, the child is gently being led to consider alternatives without feeling attacked.

One further point: As was mentioned in Chapter Two, **Destructive Cults**, cult members often adopt vocabulary and speech patterns (sometimes referred to as "loaded language") that serve to reinforce their cult beliefs. Although we encourage parents to become familiar with this vocabulary, we strongly advise against casually using it in discussions with their son or daughter, since it lends credibility to the cult jargon and often triggers associations that induce non-critical acceptance of cult doctrine. If a child uses loaded language, parents should ask for definitions and explanations in non-cult terms, as demonstrated in the sample dialogue[*] below:

> *Daughter (in cult)*: People in the outside world don't understand the true spiritual path.
> *Parent*: What do you mean by 'the outside world?'
> *Daughter*: Well, actually, it means everything outside of Guru's world.
> *Parent*: I don't know what you mean by Guru's world
> *Daughter*: It's hard to explain.
> *Parent*: Could you try to describe it in your own words?
> *Daughter*: Well, it's everything that isn't part of the lifestyle, beliefs, and teachings of our group.
> *Parent*: So when you say 'people in the outside world' you're talking about everyone who isn't a member?
> *Daughter*: Yes, I guess so.
> *Parent*: That makes me an outsider?
> *Daughter*: Well, I guess so.
> *Parent*: Why do you call it the 'outside' world?
> *Daughter*: Because it's a completely different experience of life when you follow Guru's teachings. It really is like being in a different world. Anyway, that's the term they use in the group, and it makes sense to me.
> *Parent*: Well, it's very frustrating for me.
> *Daughter*: What's frustrating?
> *Parent*: I'm trying to understand what you're saying and you use words that don't have the same meaning for both of us. For example, when you use the phrase 'outside world,' you are labeling me as an outsider, and that

---

[*] Dialogues are presented to illustrate a point, not as a script to memorize.

creates an artificial barrier between us. The way I see things, we live in one world.

Daughter: Yes, well, we do live in the same world. (Pause.) Maybe if I say "people who don't follow Guru" it will make more sense to both of us.

Bringing about such a clarification helps the daughter think of "people who don't follow Guru," many of whom she likes, rather than "everything outside Guru's world," a phrase which probably connotes "evil" and "threatening."

This section on Communication Skills offers brief, general descriptions which will be elaborated upon in the following pages. In addition, programs are available which describe and systematize communication skills in greater detail. One of these is put out by Research Press, and is entitled *Communication Workshop for Parents of Adolescents*. It has nothing to do with cults. It deals solely with communication between adolescents and adults, and it talks about different parent styles: authoritarian, in which the parent dictates to the child; inconsistent; over-protective; and the problem-solving orientation, in which problems are approached as obstacles to be understood and responded to creatively. This style resembles the approach we are describing here.

Controlling Emotional Reactions

Recognizing and learning to control emotional reactions are essential steps in establishing rapport, because these reactions can create turbulence, confusion, and distrust in a parent-child relationship.

People often have strong emotional reactions without being fully aware of what they are feeling. For example, a husband grumbles about something to his wife and she says, "What are you mad about?" and he yells back, "I'm not mad!" He may be telling an out-and-out lie, but chances are he is genuinely unaware of his feelings.

Before you can control emotions, you have to become aware of them. One way to heighten awareness is to review and try to evaluate emotional reactions from the past. In counseling parents we often suggest they keep a journal describing interactions with their child (such as telephone conversations, in-person encounters, even copies of letters sent and received) and then discuss these interactions with their spouse, family, and others with whom they have chosen to share their problem. The following are questions to consider: What did you say to your child? What did your tone of voice imply? What feelings were communicated? Anger? Hostility? Blame? Love? Respect? Understanding? Trust? Suspicion? Were there particular issues that caused you to get upset or even lose control? Why?

The above questions are intended to help parents recognize and understand their own feelings. A second area to consider is how parents' reactions may affect their relationship with their child. Getting angry, for instance, tends to have negative consequences — it often elicits defensiveness and may result in the eventual breakdown of communication, although in some situations, honest anger can shake a child out of a destructive thinking pattern. On the other hand, genuine expressions of anxiety, confusion, sadness, and disappointment tend to have positive effects, such as: helping to awaken a child's critical faculties, planting seeds of doubt about the cult, and reminding her of all that is good in the "old world." Parents can tell a child, for instance, that they are very sad that she has decided to leave school, saying "Just a few months ago you told us how much you loved school. You said it was stimulating and was giving you a chance to discover your strengths. Now you say you are leaving, and that's hard to understand. You don't seem to have your own interests in mind, and that makes us sad." Such statements are non-threatening, and may serve to strengthen feelings of love between parents and child. In some cases, the child may have similar thoughts — i.e., regret about leaving school — and be grateful for an opportunity to discuss her own feelings.

(One note of caution: We strongly advise against feigning sadness or disappointment, because such pretense often intensifies the very distrust and tension parents are trying to dispel.)

With practice, parents can learn to manage their emotions and respond constructively to their child. We often suggest that parents try to anticipate volatile situations, rehearse them mentally, and role-play them with a spouse, family member, or friend. For example: Your son is planning to come home for a few days. You might be able to anticipate or imagine likely conversations, thoughts, and feelings, such as: your son's defensiveness when he walks in the door expecting you to criticize his group and expecting to get into a heated debate, since this has occurred during numerous visits in the past; your own apprehension about getting angry, displeasing your son, saying the wrong thing, etc. As you rehearse, think about ways to improve communication, trust, and rapport, and try out different ways of responding. For example, practice listening more respectfully and asking open rather than accusatory questions.

Sample Situations to Role-Play:

Daughter tells parents: "I'm moving out of my apartment and into a monastic house with my friends from the group." Upon hearing something like this, many parents feel an immediate sense of alarm and get involved in angry debate as they try to dissuade their daughter from following through with her plans. They might threaten, "We'll disown you if you do that," or, "We're coming out to California to rescue you from that group." These reactions, though well-intentioned, may push their daughter deeper into the group. As an alternative, parents might try to communicate their anxieties in a way that does not alienate their daughter.

Cults: What Parents Should Know

Sample Dialogue:

Daughter: I'm moving out of my apartment into a monastic house with my friends from the group.

Parent: It sounds like you're considering making a very deep commitment, and it worries me.

Daughter: Why?

Parent: I'm afraid of losing the closeness we've had.

Daughter: Why? I'm just moving from one place to another in the same city.

Parent: Yes, that's true. But it seems like a giant step toward increasing your commitment to the group.

Daughter: Well, in some ways that's true.

Parent: And for us, the deeper you've gotten involved, the further away we feel, and that makes us sad.

Daughter: Well, I don't mean to push you away, but you've always criticized me.

Parent: We haven't criticized you, dear. We just don't understand the group you belong to, which frightens us. We would feel better if you communicated with us more and allowed us to share some of the important decisions in your life.

Daughter: You mean, like this decision to move?

Parent: Yes, just to talk about the pros and cons together. We want to understand your reasoning, your thinking, about the move. And we want to tell you our thoughts about it.

Son tells parents: "I want my inheritance from my grandparents. I'm over eighteen and it's legally mine." Again, parents may panic and say, "Absolutely not! You may be over eighteen, but you behave like an infant. We refuse to allow you to hand over your grandparents' gift to that slimy cult." In such a situation, parents may be legally required to give their son the money (although there may be ways of freezing the money until some later date). Whatever their response, parents should keep in mind the importance of maintaining communication and building trust. While it is sad to see money wasted, it is worse to lose touch with a child. In this type of situation, we encourage parents to invite their son home to discuss financial matters in person.

Sample Dialogue:

Son: I want my inheritance from my grandparents.

Parent: Your grandfather left you that money because he loved you. I feel very sad about your taking it now, because he would be deeply hurt if he knew what you were going to do with it.

Son: You don't trust me to use it the way you'd like me to?

Parent: No, it isn't that I don't trust you. It's just that my parents, your grandmother and grandfather, had certain hopes for you, certain ideas about how they'd like you to use the money.

Son: And they'd roll over in their graves if they knew I was giving it all to an organization that is bringing peace and fulfillment into people's lives? Aren't you projecting your own disappointment?

Parent: I admit I'm disappointed. I'm confused and worried as well. It seems that you've been rather aloof and uncommunicative lately. Now you are demanding your inheritance. We wish you would talk to us more and explain what's going on.

Son: I have tried to talk to you, but all you ever do is attack me.

Parent: We're sorry you feel that way. And we really want to try to be more understanding. But we need your help. We really would like to visit with you, so we can have a good long talk.

Son: You mean you want to set me up for a deprogramming?

Parents: No, we simply want to spend some time with you. We'll come to you. But we need some time alone with you, so we can begin to heal our family's wounds.

Child tells mother: "I'm sorry Dad is so ill and in the hospital, but I really can't come home. My work is too important." This is a particularly bad situation, first, because it indicates that the cult may have undue control over the child's life and cause her to behave in ways that she may have trouble forgiving herself for later. Second, the mother is already stressed and may not have the emotional strength to respond effectively to her daughter. At best, a parent can try to discuss the situation with the child, asking her, "Why can't you come home? Is there anything I can do to make it easier?", and honestly communicating her feelings to the child, for example, "Dad asks about you all the time. He really needs your support during this time. It's very sad that you aren't coming home." Although this is a "guilt trip," it is appropriate. Normal family decency demands some sense of guilt in such a situation.

Overcoming Barriers Produced by the Cult

Cults often use tactics which inhibit parent-child communication and erode trust. They may intentionally strive to create an emotional climate that encourages members to be more loyal to the cult than to their own families. It can be very upsetting for parents to realize that the cult has a great deal of influence while they have a very limited effect on their child. Often this frustration prompts parents to react in ways that further damage their relationship with their child. In counseling parents we try to suggest more positive ways of responding to and overcoming cult barriers.

Barrier: Limited Input
Many cults discourage members from spending time alone with their parents. Telephone calls are often supervised, with a cult member advising a child what to say. Some cults insist on sending a protective "escort" (meaning another

member) along when a child goes out with her parents or visits home. Such tactics are intended to reduce parental contact and influence.

Strategy. Although parents are handicapped, they can try to negotiate the terms of the communication. For example, a daughter calls home and says she can't come to visit on Thanksgiving. Her parents might reply angrily, "We haven't heard from you in three months. That's not fair. How do you think we feel? We raised you. We took care of you. And now this is the way you treat us?" Such an attack-type strategy often results in anger, defensiveness, and emotional distance between parents and child.

Alternately, the parents could say gently, "We are very disappointed that you haven't been coming home lately and we haven't talked. We miss you. Is there any way we can arrange to see you? Is there anything we can do? Is there anything you can do?" In this instance sadness and disappointment, but not blame, are being expressed. Parents are asking questions, asking for their daughter's ideas and indicating that they are willing to compromise and negotiate. (Of course, the style of expression — such as intonation — must be natural for the parents. Furthermore, they are including her in the search for solutions to the problem.)

Taking this a bit further, the daughter may respond with the promise, "I'll try to call home more often." If she doesn't call, then the next time her parents speak with her they might say, "We are disappointed because you told us you were going to call home more often ." Now, it is possible that she didn't call home because of cult pressures not to, and her parents' disappointment may awaken her to the cult's manipulation. She may suddenly realize that the cult is preventing her from calling, something she wants to do. She might begin to resent the control that the cult has over her life.

Barrier: Anti-Parent Propaganda
The emotional bond between parents and children is often regarded as the strongest tie that exists between human beings. Aware of the potential strength of this bond and afraid that parents will lure their children away from the group, cults may try to weaken members' ties with their families by means of anti-parent propaganda.

In one cult, for example, members are warned that "Satan works through those you love." The leader of another group coaxes, "Come to me. Your parents don't really love you. Only Guru loves you." A pseudo-Christian cult leader advises members whose parents opposed the cult, "Don't throw pearls before swine. Let the dead bury the dead. He who loves his mother and father more than me is not worthy of me." Cult members have even, on occasion, been pressured into saying they would kill their own parents should the leader ask them to. (Jim Jones had members make public declarations that they would kill any relative who opposed the People's Temple.)

Needless to say, this pitting of children against parents can have profound and devastating effects on the parent-child relationship, infusing the child with distrust, fear, even disgust for his own parents.

Strategy. The most effective means of countering anti-parent propaganda is to demonstrate, through words and actions, that what the cult says about parents simply isn't true. For example, a cult may advise new members, "When you inform your parents that you're leaving school and moving into a communal house, they will probably get very upset and angry, maybe even hysterical. Often they will yell and scream, threaten to stop supporting you, threaten to disown you. This is only because parents do not understand the beauty of our spiritual lifestyle and aspirations. Unfortunately, we can't force them to understand, and, in some cases, we may have to leave them behind."

Under these circumstances, parents who react with strong opposition are confirming the cult's predictions that "parents don't understand." As a result, the cult's credibility may be enhanced, rather than diminished, in their child's eyes.

On the other hand, if parents *don't* respond as the cult has predicted, and instead demonstrate their desire to maintain a loving, trusting, close relationship, their son or daughter might begin to wonder why the group is so negative about parents.

This is not to suggest that parents should pretend enthusiasm for the group by sending money, saying they want to be initiated, etc. Such dishonesty often breeds suspicion, while honest and gentle disagreement may stimulate a child's critical thinking and communicate parental care and concern. It *is* possible to be interested in the group without supporting it.

Barrier: Fear of Deprogramming
Cults use the deprogramming issue to aggravate members' distrust of their parents. For example, members are given exaggerated, distorted descriptions of torturous, brutal deprogramming procedures designed to "break your faith in God," procedures such as: beatings, rape, sleep deprivation, starvation. And members are warned that their parents will certainly try to deprogram them.

Strategy. If parents are not planning to deprogram their child, they are being criticized unfairly by the cult. To counter fears of deprogramming, parents can try to discuss the issue openly. For example, a daughter has refused several invitations to visit home. Her parents could say, "Are you afraid that we will try to deprogram you?" If she says "Yes," her parents could tell her that they are not planning a deprogramming and ask, "How can we reassure you?" They are being open, honest, and asking for the child's input, which gives her a sense of control over this threatening issue. They might ask her what she knows about deprogramming, and talk about the ethics involved. They could express their perceptions of her as an autonomous adult. Finally, they might ask her for suggestions as to how they could spend more time together.

Stimulating Problem-Solving Abilities

Cult members are often robbed of problem-solving opportunities. Choices about lifestyle, diet, vocation, and marriage are frequently made by the leader. Members with problems are encouraged to seek answers from the leaders or to pray, chant, or meditate until the problems disappear, or, in other words, they stop thinking about them or caring about them. Intellectual challenges are rare, and often limited to serving the cult's needs, such as administrative challenges of fundraising. Conflicting or opposing views are inaccessible or scorned, and critical thinking is denigrated as unspiritual, unnecessary, or even heretical. Finally, frequent use of mind-controlling techniques tends to inhibit or diminish problem-solving abilities, leaving many cult members at a disadvantage when it comes to using their minds to evaluate the cult.

Reevaluation of a cult commitment and critical assessment of cult practices and beliefs require the very problem-solving behavior that cults discourage, even deplore, in their members. Thus, before a cult member can address the task of reevaluation, she will often need to practice using her mind. Parents can help reawaken a child's mental abilities by: exposing her to intellectual stimulation, modeling problem-solving behavior, inviting her to participate in family problem-solving, and encouraging her to deal with and resolve personal conflicts.

Exposure to Intellectual Stimulation
Below we offer questions and suggestions to help parents determine the kind of activities that might be intellectually stimulating to their son or daughter:

- Before entering the cult, what activities did your son or daughter pursue? Reading (what type of material?); writing; watching television (which programs?); movies; theater; ballet; academic courses (what field of study?); organizational commitments (political, educational, social, professional, religious, civic, other?); games (chess, Scrabble?); travel (touring, camping, visiting friends?); art (creating, appreciating?); music (composing, playing an instrument, attending concerts?); career involvements and goals, etc. Of these activities, which seemed intellectually challenging? Which might be appealing now? How can you encourage these activities, or at least stimulate conversation about them?
- Before entering the cult, with whom did your son or daughter discuss, debate, and evaluate conflicts, beliefs, values, principles, philosophy, politics, religious views, creative ideas? (That is, friends, relatives, colleagues, teachers, counselors, co-students?) Of these people, who is currently accessible? To whom might your child respond? Might you invite them to dinner?

- Since entering the cult, has your child developed or maintained any intellectual interests? Cult-related? Non-cult related? How can you encourage the non-cult interests?
- Has your son or daughter recently expressed a desire to pursue intellectual activities — for example, schooling, reading, travel — but said there isn't any time or money to do so? How can you support these pursuits?

Once you decide upon a number of activities to suggest or make available to your child, try to incorporate them into the time he spends with you. If he rejects one suggestion, be prepared (but not overly aggressive) with another. It may take a while before you hit upon something that sparks his interest. At best, these experiences can help reactivate a cult member's critical thinking to the point where he is willing and able to reevaluate his cult commitment; at the very least, the activities will direct his attention away from the cult and towards the non-cult world.

Modeling Problem-Solving Behavior

Parents can use everyday problems to model effective problem-solving attitudes, behavior, and skills in the presence of their son or daughter. This modeling may in turn stimulate the child's own problem-solving abilities. For example:

John, a cult member, comes home to visit his parents at a time when they are trying to decide whether or not to buy a new car. Both parents have an income, contribute to the support of the family, and share responsibility for financial decisions. At this point, Dad wants to buy a car while Mom doesn't. In their effort to model problem-solving behavior, they save their discussion until mealtime, when they know John will be present.

Sample Dialogue:

Mom (to Dad): How did the car work for you today?

Dad (warm, humorously): Well, the good news is that it didn't explode. The bad news is that it needs a new exhaust system.

Mom (inviting Dad's opinion): What do you think we should do about it?

Dad (offering his opinion and voicing willingness to discuss the matter): That depends on how you look at it. I think we ought to buy a new car. But I know you disagree. What do you think?

Mom (apparently organized): Well, I've been thinking about it all day, and I made a list of financial pros and cons, including an estimate of the repairs we'd have to make on the car we have now. Here. (Shows Dad the list.)

Dad: Well, you really did your homework. I'm impressed. And your conclusion?

Mom: It seems to me that putting off buying a car for six months or so would allow us to pay off our other debts. Then we could start with a clean slate. I say get the car fixed, and buy a new one in six months. Why don't you look over my estimate and tell me what you think?

Dad: Your figures seem correct. But (voicing respectful disagreement and contributing new information) my concerns are about safety and reliability.

Frankly, I worry about driving this hunk of junk on the highway. It shakes like crazy at 45 mph. And as for reliability, I've already missed 5 or 6 important meetings because of a breakdown. It's very frustrating.

Mom (conceding her oversight): Yes, I guess I didn't consider those factors because I rarely use the car. Those are definitely serious considerations. But what about public transportation or walking? Could you manage that for a few months?

Dad (honestly): Yes, I could manage. But the truth is, I don't want to. I'd rather spend time with you and the kids than waste 2 extra hours using public transportation.

Mom: Well, I'm glad you want to spend time with us — and your newspaper! But getting back to my list, do you think we really can afford a new car?

Dad: I'm not sure, but I'd like to try to arrange our finances so that we could. Do you think we could cut expenses in other ways to compensate for a down payment?

Mom (pausing, considering): Hmmm. An interesting thought. Let's think about that possibility and discuss it tomorrow (reserving judgment and decision-making until later).

The dialogue above, while it doesn't address cult issues, does expose John to problem-solving behavior which his cult experience has denied him, such as: respect for and interest in others' opinions and feelings; willingness to seek information and to compromise; to concede error; to change one's opinion in light of rational advice; to use humor; to plan an organized, cooperative strategy, and the like.

In the cult, John had no money of his own. All his earnings as a house painter went to the cult. He was not consulted about financial decisions, even when they affected him directly. For example, when he needed a new paint brush the treasurer of the cult decided how much he could spend and where to buy it. No one asked John about his opinions or his feelings; whatever the leader told him to do, he did. Rational discussion and debate were sorely absent from his life. When John disagreed with something, he immersed himself in meditation, trying to rid himself of "negativity" (as all doubts, questions, and gripes were labeled by the cult). Finally, there were no real opportunities to problem-solve regarding personal possessions (such as a car), since members were allowed to own only the bare essentials like clothes and toothbrushes.

Involving Child in Family Problem-Solving
Another way to stimulate problem-solving is to involve a child in family decision-making. Starting with simple choices, parents might ask questions like, "What restaurant do you want to go to?"; "What movie do you want to see?"; "What color do you think we should paint the garage?"

To non-cult members, these questions may appear simplistic, even patronizing, requiring nothing more than thinking about and stating one's preferences. But for cult members, who have been taught to suppress their personal preferences, these choices may indeed be difficult, confusing, even painful. Thus, parents have to be patient, allowing their son or daughter a sufficient amount of time for a response. Although progress may seem slow or negligible, we have found that even simple questions can help stimulate a cult member's mind. In addition, by asking for his opinion, parents convey their interest, respect, and desire to include their child in family matters.

After a child becomes somewhat accustomed to making small decisions, parents might invite him to participate in more complex problem-solving, such as addressing family problems that require such skills as: considering others' thoughts, feelings, opinions, ideas; soliciting and critically evaluating relevant information; planning a cooperative strategy; drawing rational conclusions.

For example, suppose that John (from previous example) had been quite knowledgeable about cars prior to entering the cult. To involve him in family problem-solving, his parents could ask for his opinions and his reasoning regarding whether or not to buy a car. They could ask him about the safety features, performance, reliability, comfort, price, and style of various models, and, if he didn't know off-hand, ask him to help obtain information. They could invite him to visit a number of car dealers with them. They could ask for his help in planning a budget to lower their expenses for the next six months. As in other situations, parents should try to tailor their strategy to the particular abilities and interests of their son or daughter.

Encouragement to Resolve Personal Conflicts

As trust continues to build in the parent-child relationship, a cult member may begin to share some of her personal problems with her parents. She may, for instance, complain about excessive weight gain, fatigue, financial insecurity, or vocational conflicts. Without jumping in to rescue her, parents can still indicate their willingness to help and encourage their daughter to try to resolve the conflict on her own by using her own critical faculties. This can be a very delicate situation, because cult members are often told that they should resolve all their problems and satisfy their needs within the cult. Outside help, they are warned, will do more harm than good. Thus, it is crucial for parents not to impose or take over, but to carefully and caringly offer support, while encouraging critical thinking.

Sample Dialogue:

Daughter: I must have gained 25 pounds since I've been in the ashram. I'm getting fat and I don't like it.

Parent: Well, what do you expect? Your vegetarian routine is full of peanut butter, spaghetti, and the like. Why don't you quit eating that stuff and return to normal eating and normal living?

Comment. This response is likely to anger or push the child away. It places blame on the child and ridicules her eating habits and lifestyle as "not normal."

It also implies that her only choice is to leave the ashram, which may be emotionally unacceptable to her.

Alternative Dialogue:

Daughter: I must have gained 25 pounds since I've been in the ashram. I'm getting fat and I don't like it.

Parent: That's a lot of weight to gain. (Silence. Listen to daughter's response.)

Daughter: Yes, it happened so fast, I didn't even realize it. Now, none of my clothes fit me.

Parent: That must be uncomfortable for you.

Daughter: Yes, I don't know whether I should buy new clothes or go on a crash diet.

Parent: What do you think is best?

Daughter: I really don't know. I'm very frustrated about it.

Parent: That's understandable.

Daughter: I just don't seem to have the willpower I need to lose weight.

Parent: I remember when you were in high school and had a similar problem. You made a firm decision to lose weight, and succeeded. (Reminding child of personal strengths.)

Daughter: Yes, I did. I wish I could do that now. But I don't feel like I have the same control I had at that time. This is different. I don't feel like I can do it. Not alone.

Parent: Is there anything I can do to help?

Daughter: I'm not sure. Maybe if I came home, spent a week with you, I could get out of this rut of overeating.

Parent: You are welcome here anytime.

Comment. In the above conversation, the parent is careful not to tell her daughter what to do but instead to offer support. The child is leading, making her own choices, trying to solve a problem. The parent, even though she may feel the overeating is related to the cult, does not use the issue to taunt her daughter. Eventually the child may see, on her own accord, that the cult lifestyle and diet are in large part responsible for her weight gain. *Or,* parents might suggest this connection in a non-threatening, non-ridiculing way when their daughter seems ready and able to hear it. This may lead to a friendly yet critical discussion of the group's dietary beliefs — which in turn could lead to critical discussions of other aspects of the group.

Chapter Eight

Understanding Cult Influence

One of the main goals of promoting voluntary reevaluation is to help a cult member make an autonomous, informed choice between the cult and the non-cult world. This requires: (1) understanding and critically assessing cult and non-cult influences; (2) reevaluating the non-cult world; and, eventually, (3) making a choice between the two. This chapter offers practical suggestions for evaluating a cult's influence.

Once parents have established rapport, overcome some of the cult barriers to communication, and stimulated their child's problem-solving abilities, it is a good time to begin *directly addressing cult issues* with their son or daughter.

Talking about the cult is bound to create tension and arouse a child's defensiveness. Parents should anticipate this and try to be sensitive to their child's feelings, remembering that the intent is not to bully a child into leaving, but to provide a setting conducive to reevaluating affiliation with the cult. Patience and discretion are invaluable assets here. For example, if, in the midst of a discussion a child becomes reticent, sullen, suspicious, enraged, etc., it may be wise to back off and wait until his mood is more receptive. This is not to suggest avoidance of all conflict, but rather that parents must evaluate whether the continuation of a particular discussion is constructive or not. Also, there may be times when parents, feeling ill-prepared to respond constructively to a child's comments about the cult, want to put off a discussion until they feel more knowledgeable.

In their discussions about the cult, we suggest that parents focus on the three major forces of cult influence: Manipulation, Repulsion, and Attraction.

Manipulation

Manipulation refers to the unethically (that is, deceptive, coercive) persuasive tactics cults use on their members, on potential converts, and on society at large, including but not limited to: false promises, misrepresentation, suppression of doubts, group pressure, techniques to overwhelm reason, isolation from non-cult influence, and control of daily activities.

Cult members are often genuinely unaware of the cult's manipulative ploys. Or, they may have an arsenal of rationalizations which excuse, defend, or even exalt the tactics (for example, "We're lying for God."). Believing that they have freely chosen to commit themselves to the group, members do not realize that manipulative forces played a major role in their recruitment and indoctrination and continue to influence them to remain in the group. Furthermore, members often don't recognize their own use of manipulation to recruit and indoctrinate others.

In our counseling work, we encourage parents to become familiar with the manipulative tactics being used on their child by thoroughly reviewing all the information they have gathered thus far — from reading, visiting the cult, talking with child and others, and the like. Once parents understand the cult's unethical manipulation, they can *then* begin to help their child recognize and evaluate these practices.

Sample Dialogue: Cult Manipulation:

Parent: How does somebody actually become a member of The—— (cult name)?

Child: It varies from person to person. It's not premeditated.

Parent: What about for you? How did you become interested in the first place?

Child: Why do you want to know?

Parent: Well, you've been involved with the group for almost a year now, and I never asked you exactly how it began.

Child: Are you interested in joining?

Parent: I'm interested in you.

Child: Well, if you really want to know, there was something very special about the man who started talking to me at college.

Parent: What did he tell you?

Child: It wasn't what he said, but the way he treated me. He was decent. Straightforward. Happy.

Parent: He must have mentioned something about The——, though?

Child: No. Not the first time we talked. He just seemed to have spiritual interests.

Parent: But do you think his goal was to get you to come to a meeting?

Child: Well, not really. I think at first he was just being friendly. Sharing. When he saw I was interested in spiritual things also, he offered to go with me to a meeting.

Parent: Is it possible that he wanted to interest you in the group all along?

Child: (Defensively) Yes, but what's wrong with that?

Parent: (Backing off, reflecting question back to child): What do you think about it? (Pause) Is there anything wrong with concealing your motives?

Child: (Firmly) Sometimes it's all right!

Parent: (Quietly) I'm not sure what you mean.

Child: (Silent, then shares confidence with parent) You see, if it's for a good cause, then it is all right. Because sometimes if you tell people right away, they reject the whole thing. But if they trust you first, then you can tell them and they'll really listen.

Parent: (Non-judgmental, expressing own feelings) I would feel dishonest doing that.

Child: (Sharing own feelings) Well, sometimes I feel a little uncomfortable doing it.

Parent: (Pausing, letting child digest the import of her statement; then, caringly) Then why do you do it?

Child: (Silent for a minute, then) I guess because I believe in The——. I really want people to find out about it.

Parent: No matter what the means?

Child: Well, no. I wouldn't go to an extreme. I'd just try to find the best way to help a person understand how special The—— is.

Parent: (Shifting focus back to manipulation used on child.) Is it possible that the man who recruited you felt that way?

Child: I'm sure he did.

Parent: Still, that would upset me, if someone used such indirect means to get me to come to a meeting.

Child: Well, I felt a little upset at first, but only because I wanted to go out with him. He was very attractive.

Parent: (Sympathetically) That must have been disappointing.

Child: At first, yes. But it was worth it. I got so much more from the group than a relationship could ever give me.

Parent: (Confirming and accepting child's statement) Yes, I know you feel you've gained a lot from the group. (Then, gently) It's just hard for me to understand how you can accept a dishonest approach.

Child: (Defensively) I never said dishonesty was good. You're twisting my words around to fit your own diagnosis! (Escalating anger) That's the trouble with you. You just don't understand. You'll never understand!

Parent: (Pausing until child is finished, then, non-defensively) Is there anything you can think of that might help? Something I could do?

Child: (Expected parent's anger, is nonplussed, pauses for a moment, then) Well, maybe if you came to a meeting? (Child expects refusal.)

Parent: I really want to understand, so I'll go with you to a meeting.

Child: (Astounded) You'll come to a meeting?

Parent: Yes, but I'd like to negotiate a deal — I'll go to the meeting, but in return I'd like a little more time alone with you, like today, to talk privately, so that I *can* understand. (Up until now, child has only come home for day visits.)

Child: (Suspiciously) Wait a minute. What are you talking about, being alone with me? I'm alone with you now. Do you want me to spend the rest of my life here with you, discussing The——? If so, forget it!

Parent: (Concerned) I'm sorry. Maybe I wasn't clear. (Pause)

Child: (Impatiently) Well, what *do* you want?

Parent: I think we both want the same thing (Pause), to understand each other.

Cults: What Parents Should Know

Child: Yes, but you know I can't spend too much time away from the group, even if you do come to a meeting.

Parent: How much time could you spend?

Child: I'm not sure. I'd have to talk to the people there first, and explain the situation.

Parent: What do you think they'll say?

Child: (Sharing confidence with parent) Probably that I shouldn't spend much time with you.

Parent: But what are your feelings? What do you want to do?

Child: I don't know.

Parent: You know, I feel very frustrated.

Child: Why?

Parent: Because it seems like our relationship is dependent on the group.

Child: (Pauses, then): It's true, my first commitment is to The——. It's very important to me. And I feel an obligation to check with them about taking time off.

Parent: I respect your feelings of obligation. But one thing troubles me. It seems as though they're very suspicious about parents without even finding out what the particular parents are like. I feel like I'm being judged unfairly.

Child: (Defending group): How can you blame them? Most parents would deprogram their kids if they could. (Pause)But it's true, you promised you wouldn't try deprogramming me. They know that. (Pause, then quietly, almost to herself): I wonder why they're still so negative about my visiting you?

Parent: That must be frustrating for you, too?

Child: Yes.

Parent: Is there anything you could do, or we could do, to change that?

Child: (Cautiously): Well, I could just tell them, instead of asking them, that I was going to spend time alone with you, and that in return you'd come to some meetings.

Parent: I'd be very happy if you would do that, and I'll support you in any way I can. And I look forward to fulfilling my end of the bargain.

Child: Thanks, Mom.

Comment. The dialogue above illustrates how conversation can help awaken a child to such cult manipulations as deception in the recruitment process, unfair generalizations about parents, and undue control over members' lives (with regard, for example, to decision-making and relationships with family). Of course, this is a *sample* conversation, and the child feels close enough to her mother to express some doubts about the cult. Often such a dialogue can only take place after months or even years of work on the parent-child relationship.

From the cult member's perspective, acknowledging manipulation may be difficult, disturbing, even painful. Members who heretofore believed in the infallibility, the scrupulous practice and beliefs, and the innate goodness of the cult will require time and support to face the deflated reality. Therefore, conversations such as the above should be well-timed, low-key, and at first aimed simply at raising questions in the child's mind.

Once a child seems able to openly acknowledge and question the cult manipulation, additional resources can be offered to help confirm, clarify, and strengthen a child's understanding, such as:

- Literature concerning manipulation
- People who have experience with cult manipulation such as: former members of The——, former member of other cults.

Repulsion

Repulsion is a second type of cult influence, referring to those aspects of the cult which are distasteful, disturbing, or otherwise unpleasant for a member. Loneliness, boredom, exhaustion, dislike for other members, corruption in the upper ranks, lack of privacy, crowded and unsanitary living conditions, and strictures barring the pursuit of personal goals (such as education, career, intimacy) are potential sources of doubt and discontent which could push a member towards leaving the cult.

But cult members, as noted earlier, are specifically instructed to repress, dismiss, deny, or overcome any misgivings they may have about the group (for example, "Meditate, and your doubts will disappear."; "A perfect devotee will have perfect faith, and no questions!"; "Doubts are the workings of Satan."; "Put your questions in your back pocket and sit on them!") In addition, if a member's doubts persist, she is warned to keep them strictly within the confines of the group. Never, ever, is a member supposed to confess her doubts to outsiders.

As a result of such inhibitive warnings, repulsive factors may hover in the remote background of a member's awareness throughout her cult years. However, parents can help awaken a child to repulsive factors by providing a safe environment in which doubts can be expressed freely. Below are some suggestions for establishing such an environment.

Do's and Don'ts for Creating a "Safe" Environment

- **DO** be patient. As trust is established, your child will be more prone to share some of his misgivings about the group.
- **DO** listen supportively, encouraging your child to explore her doubts further, and letting her know that you sympathize and understand.
- **DO** express your appreciation that your child is trusting enough to confide in you.
- **DO** let your child form his own opinions and come to his own conclusions (saying, for example, "Now that you've told us about the corruption in the leadership, what do you think?"). In some cases, you may think your

child's conclusions are foolish. You don't have to agree, and you certainly can present your reasons, but remember that informed, voluntary reevaluation should allow the child to form opinions different from those of his parents.

- **DO** be open to the possibility that some of your own conclusions are wrong.
- **DO** allow your child to express positive feelings about the cult and cult members.
- **DON'T** pressure your child to voice her doubts about the cult by saying, for example, "Come on, Kathy, we know you have doubts about the M—— (cult). Why don't you just speak up and stop holding back?") This approach puts the child on the defensive.
- **DON'T** exploit a child's doubts just to prove you are right (as when your child complains that he doesn't get any privacy in the K——(cult) and you respond, "You see, we were right. We told you so. We told you that you'd be unhappy in that group.") This only serves to humiliate him.
- **DON'T** put words in a child's mouth, or make judgments about the cult for her (for example, "Jane, you know that the group you are in is a destructive cult.") This will make it more difficult for her to voice her own opinions.
- **DON'T** blame the other cult members for your child's unhappiness (by saying, for example, "Ed, those people don't care about you. They are using you for your time and money.") First of all, this statement is generally untrue. With the exception of a select few who, along with the leader, may engage in intentional exploitation of members, there is often a sincere bond of friendship and loyalty among fellow cultists. Second, it may be threatening for a child to hear his parents criticize the members. If he has misgivings, he will feel safer if he is the one to initiate the discussion and place the blame.
- **DON'T** blame your child for being naive or slow to criticize the cult. Remember, she may not be intentionally ignoring the facts. She may as yet be unable to critically assess the group.
- If at all possible, **DON'T** interrupt him while he is speaking. Allow him to finish expressing himself before interjecting your own ideas. This will communicate respect for him and provide you with a fuller understanding of his thoughts and feelings.
- **DO** address your child personally, and not as a representative of the cult. For example, asking "What has meditation been like for you?", will direct a child's attention toward her personal experiences, while asking, "What is meditation?" may prompt a rote-type answer and make her feel more like a cult representative.
- **DO** allow for some silence in the midst of a discussion. Although sometimes awkward, silence permits and often promotes introspection, a necessary ingredient for critical evaluation. If parents can be comfortably silent, the child is more likely to feel safe taking the time to reflect during a discussion.

- **DO** be prepared to end a dialogue without coming to a definite conclusion, especially when a child seems to have had enough talking for a while. This is not to say that parents shouldn't encourage exploration; rather, it is a reminder that too much pressure may cause withdrawal. The balance is a delicate one.

Note: The above DO'S and DON'TS are guidelines and not rules, and parents are advised to remain flexible and responsive to their own unique situations. Occasionally interrupting a child in mid-sentence, or blurting out a derogatory remark about the cult, are not terrible mistakes, and can be easily corrected with a simple apology or an acknowledgment that the comments were impulsive.

In preparation for discussing repulsive aspects of the cult, parents should first review their information about the group and familiarize themselves with potentially repulsive factors (by asking, for example: are members generally overworked? denied intimacy? living under unsanitary conditions?). Second, thinking over past conversations with their child, parents should try to recall any hints of dissatisfaction with the cult (remembering, for example, whether a child may have mentioned, in passing, her dislike for some of the members). Keeping this information in mind, parents can try to focus the discussions on those repulsive factors which are particularly relevant to their child's cult experiences.

In the following dialogue the son has taken the initiative to express and explore his doubts with his father.

Sample Dialogue Regarding Cult Repulsion:

Son: I've noticed that my body isn't as rugged as it used to be.
Dad: Oh?
Son: Actually, I haven't felt healthy in a long time.
Dad: I'm glad you could tell me, and I'm sorry you don't feel good.
Son: Yes, well, sometimes I wonder if I may be getting really sick.
Dad: How so? Is there anything Mom or I could do to help?
Son: Well, I don't know. I've been working long hours and not getting much sleep.
Dad: If I were in your situation, what with all the time you spend working at the store (cult business), I imagine I would be totally exhausted.
Son: Yes, that's it. I am exhausted. (Pause, then, tentatively) You know, the only time I really feel rested is when I'm home with you. The people at the (cult) Center don't seem to understand how I feel.
Dad: You wish they would show more concern for you?
Son: Yes, that does bother me.
Dad: As though your health wasn't very important?
Son: Well, yes. (Pauses, then, feeling guilty for expressing negative thoughts about his cult friends, proceeds to defend them.) But don't get me wrong, those people are very special to me. Really, they're my best friends in the

world. It's just, well, everyone seems overworked, and that makes it hard to consider anyone else's problems.

Dad: Why do you think that's happening?

Son: I'm not sure, except that there's a lot of pressure.

Dad: What kind of pressure?

Son: In a sense, we pressure one another. When I see someone working very hard to bring in new people, I feel that I should push myself more.

Dad: Like being in a highly competitive environment?

Son: Yes, it is competitive, in a way. But it shouldn't be that way. (Son has made his own judgment.) We're working towards a spiritual goal. And competition is such a materialistic concept.

Dad: I'm still not sure why you work so hard to recruit people.

Son: (Offers rote-like answer) Basically, we want the world to know about S—
—(cult).

Dad: But to work to the point of exhaustion?

Son: There is something exhilarating about putting your mind, body, and soul to work for a good cause.

Dad: Yes, I can understand the excitement in that, especially in my work with handicapped children. But I try to watch out for my own health. I can't help children if I'm sick.

Son: (Rote-like defensive answer) My health is secondary to spreading the good word.

Dad: Just what do you mean by that? I've heard you say it before, but I'm not sure I really understand. And this worries and saddens me.

Son: (Touched, feels safer, confides his feelings) I guess I'm not sure I meant that. To be honest with you, I am worried about myself, and I'm tired of pretending it doesn't matter.

Dad: Why pretend?

Son: (Confides) Guru says that the best devotee is the one who doesn't care about himself.

Dad: What do you think?

Son: I don't know. (Pauses, then) I want to live up to Guru's advice, but it's not always easy.

Dad: That must create some tension for you?

Son: Yes, but (defensive) tension is part of life.

Dad: That's true. I guess what troubles me is how far you might go in following his advice.

Son: What do you mean?

Dad: Well, what do you think you would do if the Guru asked you to do something that wasn't good for you?

Son: I don't know. (Pauses, then gives a rote response) We don't always know what's best for us.

Dad: I agree. And yet, is it possible that the Guru doesn't have your best interests in mind?

Son: (Momentarily taken aback, but then attempts to express confidence) Oh, I know he does.

Dad: I know the Guru is important to you. Still, if someone suggested that my health wasn't important, I would feel as though he didn't care about me.

Son: Yes, but these aren't normal circumstances. Guru isn't just someone. He's my spiritual teacher.

Dad: It's hard to evaluate him by ordinary standards?

Son: I guess the truth of the matter is, I don't really evaluate him at all. I just accept him.

Dad: And yet, now that you are sick, it creates a conflict. What do you think you should do?

Son: I don't know.

Dad: Have you ever considered that maybe the Guru isn't the right spiritual teacher for you?

Son: How can you say that, knowing how important he is to me?

Dad: I'm looking at you as your father, and I can see that you're not well. It frightens me to think you're following the advice of someone who tells you your health isn't important. If it was your son, how do you think you would react?

Son: (Silent for a moment) I've never thought about it from that perspective. (Pauses) I might be upset, just like you are. I really don't know.

Dad: I am terribly concerned about you. I've never seen you so tired and pale.

Son: (Resorting to rote response): Guru takes care of us.

Dad: You may or may not agree, but I think that a father's love for his child is one of the most spiritual feelings a human being can have. (Sensing that it is time to give his son space) Please think about what we've just discussed.

Son: Okay, Dad.

Dad: Thanks.

Comment. From the very beginning of this dialogue the son seems to be asking for a forum to express (1) his negative feelings about the cult — the exhausting, competitive environment, and the resulting indifference of members toward one another; and (2) his need for sympathy, understanding, and perhaps even medical attention. However, he is apparently ambivalent about exposing his feelings to his father, as evidenced in his fluctuating complaints and praises for the cult. This fluctuation is common in cultists trying to express their doubts. Note that in praising the cult the son reverts to rote-like comments and generalizations, and often employs the collective term "we."

In response, the father:

- Acknowledges that he regards his son's health as an important concern.
- Shows sympathy and concern, but doesn't blame the cult or the leader, and doesn't rush in to rescue his son.
- Instead, he offers to participate in problem-solving: "Is there anything you could do, or we could do, to help?"
- Models appropriate responses by putting himself hypothetically into his son's situation: "I imagine I would be totally exhausted." "If someone suggested that my health wasn't important, I would feel like he didn't care about me."

- Uses *questions* to help his son clarify his feelings and define the situation, allowing room for the son to refute or accept his father's analysis without getting defensive. He says, for example: "You wish they would show more concern for you?" "As though your health wasn't important?" "Like being in a highly competitive environment?" "That must create some tension for you?" "It's hard to evaluate him by ordinary standards?"
- Encourages critical analysis by asking son to consider hypothetical situations: "What do you think you would do if the Guru asked you to do something that wasn't good for you?" "Is it possible that the Guru doesn't have your best interests in mind?" "If it were your son, how do you think you would react?"

By the end of the dialogue, the son has not only expressed some of his negative feelings about the cult, but he has also accepted from his father the love and concern that was sorely missing from the cult environment. Even though he continues to defend the group, his father has caused him to begin thinking in a more open, critical way.

Attraction

Attraction is the third type of cult influence, referring to those aspects of the cult which a child feels are beneficial. Common sources of attraction include companionship; appeal of cult doctrine (for example, its seeming universality); control over destructive habits (such as smoking, drinking, or drug abuse); promises of immortality and salvation; acquisition of new skills (such as cooking, sales, accounting, carpentry, public speaking, leadership and administrative abilities); a sense of purpose in life; no worldly commitments; minimal responsibility for making practical and ethical decisions; elitist status; feeling independent from one's parents; periods of ecstasy, happiness, or peace; and following a charismatic leader.

In helping a son or daughter understand and assess cult attractions, parents should remember that *cult involvement is not a totally negative experience.* In addition to many pleasurable feelings, members often acquire skills and wisdom during their cult years which prove to be valuable assets after they leave the cult. Acknowledging these positive aspects is one way parents can help a child recognize that the time she spent in the cult was not wasted. And should she decide to leave the cult, these positive memories can help temper some of the disappointment and lack of confidence that often trouble former cult members.

In light of the harm cults can inflict on members, parents often find it extremely difficult to acknowledge any benefits their child may have reaped from her experience. However, by overemphasizing the negative and denying the positive, parents are being both unrealistic and unfair to their child, and perpetuate the cult notion that "parents don't understand." While we certainly don't expect parents to praise the cult, we do suggest sincere acceptance of those aspects which are essentially positive.

In the dialogues below, we offer practical examples of how parents can acknowledge the plusses of c··lt involvement and help a child evaluate cult attractions, noting that some   :eal while others are specious.

Acknowledging the Plusses

Sample Dialogue: Acknowledging the Plusses
Setting: Daughter visits home after attending a weekend cult festival.

Mother: How was the festival?
Daughter: I had such a fantastic time!
Mother: I'm glad. I'd like to hear about your experiences.
Daughter: I felt like I was on a rejuvenating vacation.
Mother: That sounds lovely. What did you do?
Daughter: (Tentative) Well, it might not sound so wonderful to you. You'd have to have been there to really understand.
Mother: It's true that you and I may have different ideas about what is rejuvenating. But I'm still interested in hearing about things that are pleasurable for you.
Daughter: (Still tentative) Okay, well, first of all, there were 15,000 people there from all over the world.
Mother: An international gathering.
Daughter: Yes.
Mother: How was everyone accommodated?
Daughter: It was amazing how smoothly everything went. People slept in tents and we all ate together in this huge dining tent.
Mother: And was there some sort of organized program?
Daughter: Yes, we listened to speakers and music, mostly.
Mother: What was special about the festival for you?
Daughter: It's a tremendous, powerful feeling when so many people from different countries come together in a common bond.
Mother: It feels as though you're part of something significant?
Daughter: Yes, it really does.
Mother: I can understand that. In fact, I had similar feelings when I participated in a civil rights demonstration twenty years ago.

Comment. In this dialogue the mother does not praise or even condone her daughter's cult involvement. Instead, she simply acknowledges that her daughter had a positive experience and subtly suggests that similar positive experiences can occur outside the cult, thereby setting the stage for further discussion.

Evaluating Cult Attractions: Are They Real or Specious?
That which appears good or feels good may not be good. This is especially so

in destructive cults, where infatuating promises often obscure members' awareness of the more somber, underlying reality. Through dialogue, parents can help a child determine whether cult attractions are substantive or specious, beneficial or harmful, ethical or corrupt. For example, we could continue the above dialogue about the cult festival thus:

Sample Dialogue: Evaluating Cult Attractions (continued from the previous dialogue):

Daughter: Yes, I remember you telling me about that demonstration. Wasn't Dr. Martin Luther King there?

Mother: Yes, that's right.

Daughter: I've heard that it was very exciting. I guess you can relate to my experience, then?

Mother: I think I can, but I'd like to hear more. Were there other special aspects of the festival? (At this point mother has the option of elaborating on her civil rights experience as a comparison to the cult experience. In this example, however, mother chooses to seek more information.)

Daughter: Well, yes. Guru was there. We heard him speak. (Pauses, then, hesitantly) And we had a chance to kiss his feet.

Mother: (Gently, without judgment) Now that's something I have a hard time imagining. What was that like for you?

Daughter: It's hard to describe. (Pause) Well, it's just very blissful.

Mother: Blissful?

Daughter: It's like, all year long we go about our lives, meditating, working, going to meetings, all that. But once a year we get to see Guru. It's like, we've been looking forward to that experience all year, and when it actually happens, it's very moving.

Mother: (Tries to further clarify daughter's description) There's a certain expectation of what's going to happen when you kiss his feet?

Daughter: Well, yes. There's both an expectation and a hope — the hope that we'll feel a deep connection with Guru.

Mother: What kind of connection?

Daughter: A feeling of love and surrender, like people feel when they're making love, except that with Guru, it's a purer experience.

Mother: What makes it pure?

Daughter: Well, Guru himself is pure.

Mother: I'm not sure what you mean.

Daughter: He is beyond desire; he isn't trying to fulfill any personal needs.

Mother: How does he show that?

Daughter: He doesn't have to, because we have faith in him.

Mother: In a sense, then, you see him as more than a human being?

Daughter: Yes, that's right, to me he is the embodiment of God.

Mother: What kind of person is he, that brings you to worship him?

Daughter: Actually, I don't know much about him personally. My relationship with him is more on a spiritual level.

Mother: There must be something about him, though, that fits your criteria for God?

Daughter: Just a deep inner feeling that I trust. (Pause) I feel happiest when I'm near him.

Mother: (Gently persistent) He must be doing something special?

Daughter: No, not really. It's just that being near him is a wonderful experience.

Mother: (Tries to get daughter to think about cause and effect) If it isn't anything he does, do you think your expectations might have something to do with how wonderful it is?

Daughter: (Defensive) You mean, do I think I'm imagining the whole experience?

Mother: (Gently) No, not so much imagining. I recognize that your experience is real. What I mean is, is it possible that your experience with Guru comes more from what you and the other followers anticipate than from the Guru himself?

Daughter: (Outraged) That's ridiculous! I could never fabricate such beautiful, intense experiences, not even during my most creative moments! (Pause) What are you trying to do? Ruin my experience? Discredit Guru?

Mother: (Tries to re-establish rapport) I'm sorry you feel that way. (Shifts to her own experience) I'm trying to put myself in your shoes and understand why you believe Guru is God. It's hard for me to understand.

Daughter: What's so hard about it? I just have faith in him. It's that simple.

Mother: I guess I would react differently. (Shifts focus to herself)

Daughter: (Intrigued) In what way?

Mother: Well, first of all, I'd want to know what kind of a person he was. I wouldn't trust my feelings completely.

Daughter: Why not?

Mother: Because sometimes my feelings lead me astray.

Daughter: How?

Mother: Well, I never told you this story, but before I met your father, I was dating a married man.

Daughter: (Somewhat incredulous) You didn't know he was married, did you?

Mother: Well, yes and no. On a factual level, I did know. But emotionally I was so attracted to him, the feeling was so strong, that I literally convinced myself that we belonged together. In a sense, I was blinded by my feelings.

Daughter: Wow, I never knew that about you.

Mother: I'm glad I could tell you. It was a difficult time for me. And very humbling. Up until then, I believed I could trust my feelings completely. And that's why I believe anyone could be overwhelmed by feelings.

Daughter: Including me, I suppose.

Mother: Yes, that's what I'm thinking.

Daughter: Well, I don't know. It's true that I believe in Guru because of my feelings. But sometimes feelings are accurate. (Pauses) I guess you're saying that sometimes feelings can be wrong?

Mother: Or at least overshadow some of the facts. What do you think?

Daughter: (Somewhat perturbed) I guess it's possible. I haven't thought about it very much. But I don't think that's the case with Guru. I'm sure I would be able to tell if something was wrong, if I was headed in a bad direction.

Mother: If I were in your situation, I think it would be very hard for me to re-examine my feelings about the Guru from a critical perspective. In a way, I wouldn't want to know, or even consider, that something might be wrong. (By placing herself in daughter's situation, mother can suggest a reluctance to think critically without accusing her daughter of anything.)

Daughter: Why?

Mother: Having dedicated my life to what seemed like a good person and a good cause, I'd be afraid of the disappointment. (Tries to bring daughter's fears out in the open)

Daughter: If something were wrong, let's say Guru turned out to be a phoney, do you honestly think I would purposely overlook that fact just to avoid disappointment?

Mother: (Turns question back to daughter) What do you think?

Daughter: Well, for one, I can't imagine him being a phony. But no, I'd be true to myself. I wouldn't follow a false God.

Mother: But how would you know whether he was true or false?

Daughter: (Perturbed) I don't know. A few minutes ago I would have said I could tell by the way I felt. Now I'm not sure. (Pauses) Mom, how do *you* figure out what's true? (Note: It is unusual for a cult member to ask her parent for advice on discerning the truth. This indicates the daughter's willingness to question her own perceptions.)

Mother: I don't have any easy answer. (Gently) One thing I know is that it can be very upsetting to think critically about someone we love. (Tries to anticipate daughter's feelings, and uses the inclusive term "we" to indicate shared feelings and sharing of the problem)

Daughter: I feel kind of guilty even talking about this. I do love Guru, and I've never questioned him. I can't conceive of doubting him now. He means too much to me.

Mother: (Sympathetic): I understand. I know he means the world to you. I felt that way, too. (Hugs daughter. Silence while mother and daughter embrace, then...) I don't think it's a betrayal to want to be honest with ourselves.

Comment. In this dialogue, the daughter comes to recognize (1) feelings aren't always enough to discern truth, and, in some instances, can overshadow important facts; (2) she isn't sure whether her feelings about the Guru prove he is really God; and (3) thinking critically about someone you love (in this case, Guru) is not a betrayal; on the contrary, it can help you to be honest with yourself. With this heightened awareness she can, with encouragement, begin to critically *assess* specific cult attractions.

To determine the specific attractions a cult holds for their child, parents should remain alert for relevant comments he or she makes about the group. In addition, they can ask their child questions such as: What was special for you about the festival? What is special about the group? About the leader? About the philosophy? About the lifestyle? About the meditation? Are there positive changes you see in yourself since joining the group? What are they? Positive changes in others? Does the group engage in projects or activities that are geared to help people? Members? Non-members? Both?

We are not suggesting an interrogation session, but simply an occasional question to express interest in the child and to elicit helpful information. Also, we caution parents to remember that the task is not to show a child that everything she thought was good about the cult is bad; it is to help her discern which attractions *are* good and which are specious, unethical, or harmful. Another goal is to help the child see that most of the benefits can be achieved in the mainstream world. A gentle parental attitude can help soften the pain of re-evaluation, making the process more bearable for a child. Note how, in the above dialogue, the mother repeatedly acknowledges how difficult this process can be.

Finally, in addressing cult attractions, former members of the cult can offer valuable insight both for the parents and for the child (if and when she is willing to speak with them).

Chapter Nine

Assessing the Non-Cult World

Assessing the non-cult world is an important and parallel task to evaluating cult influence. If a member is to leave a cult voluntarily, he must feel both the need to withdraw from the cult (as less attractive) and the desire to return to the outside world (as more attractive).

In our counseling work we have found that one of the most anxiety-producing aspects of leaving a cult is the prospect of facing the non-cult world. There are two basic reasons for this anxiety: (1) cult-induced repulsion towards the outside world, and (2) unresolved, non-cult-related anxieties which members brought with them when they entered the cult. It is often these negative feelings towards the outside world, even more than the positive feelings they have towards the cult, that keep members from leaving.

Through discussion and practical experience, parents can help a child test the reality of the outside world, helping him overcome both cult-induced repulsion and non-cult-related anxieties. In addition, they can systematically work to remind her about the genuine attractions — frequently denigrated by the cult — of the non-cult world.

Cult-Induced Repulsion

As noted earlier, cults can be quite adept at alienating members from the mainstream of society. They can sow seeds of distrust, contempt, fear, intolerance, and indifference towards people and events outside the group. They can isolate members from non-cult influences so that they are unable to test cult depictions of the world against the actual reality. And they can denigrate those things outside the group which members find attractive (for example, intimacy, education, career, family, religion, sports, other personal interests).

To counter cult-induced repulsion, parents should first become familiar with the specific approach — language, philosophy, attitude, and practical posture — the cult takes towards the outside world. Cult literature and tapes, and cult meetings (if parents decide to attend) may provide some clues. Next, parents should try to ascertain how their child perceives the world, listening for relevant remarks and, when appropriate, asking questions, such as: Are you interested in continuing your education? Have you considered returning to college? Why/why not? Do you have any plans for a career? If yes, what are they? If not, how about discussing the issue? Are you thinking at all about getting married? Having a family? Would you like to go out with a woman who is interested in meeting you (for example, a friend's daughter)? Do you have any money put away for yourself for the future? Would you like to go to temple/church with us this weekend?

When they have obtained adequate information, parents can initiate discussions to help their son or daughter reevaluate the non-cult world. During such discussions parents need not, and should not pretend that the non-cult world is a bed of roses. For a child to function in that world, he needs and deserves an honest appraisal. The truth of the matter is, there *is* evil, greed, hatred, and the like, in the world. And like it or not, some, even many, of the negative things cults say are true. What cults fail to do, however, is recognize any *good* in the world. This ongoing presentation of half-truths often succeeds in creating a vilified image of the world beyond the cult "shelter."

It is possible, and constructive, to acknowledge the more troubling aspects of non-cult life, while still affirming its positive qualities. In fact, cult members can learn a great deal, and even become less fearful about leaving the cult, when parents model or describe their way of handling unpleasant life situations.

Sample Dialogue for Helping a Child Assess Cult-Induced Repulsion:
Setting: Son comes home to visit for the weekend. Father and son have just been reading the newspaper over breakfast.

Son: Reading this newspaper, I can see how lucky I am. Being part of N—— (cult name) has really protected me from this crazy world. I don't know how I could possibly live in this world.

Dad: (Confirming son's feelings) I know there are a lot of troubling things going on in the world. (Then seeks more detail.) But I'm not sure what you mean by craziness.

Son: Well, materialism, for one thing. People are constantly grabbing, stealing, stepping on each other, trying to acquire more and more things, more and more money. They're worse than animals. I think that's disgusting.

Dad: Yes, I think that sometimes human beings can be very disappointing. It sounds as though you've had some pretty upsetting experiences with people.

Son: Well, (pauses, then—) absolutely! Every day I see people on the bus, on the streets, in the stores, who are callous toward one another. Just the other day I watched hundreds of people pass by this homeless woman. She was lying outside in the bitter cold, on a park bench, huddled under her coat. And no one stopped to help.

Dad: You must have felt a strong urge to help her.

Son: (Sheepish) Well, yes, I really wanted to do something. (In a very small voice) But I didn't do anything.

Dad: You wish you had done something to help?

Son: Yes. I feel like a hypocrite, complaining about the world being indifferent and then acting this way. (Pauses) Dad, what would you have done in that situation?

Dad: I'm not sure. I might have called the police. They have a new policy that allows them to bring homeless people to shelters.

Son: I didn't know that, about the shelters. That's a good idea. I'm surprised they came up with something so humane. I just figured those people froze to death.

Dad: Yes, it gives me a good feeling about our city, a sense that people do care. (Voices own feelings without lecturing son)

Son: But don't you think that in general people are oblivious to each other's pain?

Dad: What prompts you to say that?

Son: (Pauses) I don't know. I just have this gut feeling that if I were really in trouble, if I really needed help, let's say I was being mugged on the street, that no one would stop to help.

Dad: It sounds like you don't have much confidence in human beings.

Son: That's true. I am kind of pessimistic about people.

Dad: That makes me sad.

Son: Why?

Dad: Because although there's an ugly side to people, there's a beautiful side, too. And it makes me sad to think that you're missing out on the good part.

Son: Well, I'm not really missing out. I feel very positive about people in N——.

Dad: That leaves out a majority of the human population, including me.

Son: (Momentarily embarrassed) I'm sorry, I didn't mean to include you. It's just that I think people in N—— are special, different from other people.

Dad: How?

Son: Well, for example, they don't hoard things to themselves. They're not striving for material gains. Everything is owned by the group. It's like a family, except that no one is related by blood. I think that's kind of exceptional, a group of unrelated people sharing their money and caring for each other like family. Where else could you find people doing that? (Note: People in cults often think their lifestyle and ideals are entirely unique.)

Dad: If I was in N——, I'd probably feel that I was participating in something unique.

Son: Yes, I do feel that way. But I wish the rest of the world was more like us.

Dad: I'm not sure what you mean.

Son: Well, idealistic, caring, and sharing their possessions with others.

Dad: You feel most people are selfish?

Son: Yes, don't you?

Dad: I think that different people have different ways of showing that they care.

Son: Like what?

Dad: Well, take charity as an example. I can think of a number of charitable organizations whose sole purpose is to help people. Your mother and I have a little extra money every month, and we donate some of it to charity. The money is used to help people in need, people we don't even know.

Son: But these charities, how do you know the money is really going where they say? How do you know it's not a front for a few businessmen to get rich?

Dad: It's true that some groups may misuse the money they get. But all of the charities I support are required to print a financial report. And if I wanted to volunteer my time, I could participate in the helping process and personally witness how the money was being spent.

Son: Oh, I didn't realize it was so easy to find out.

Dad: Yes, I guess you're not that familiar with the procedures of charitable organizations?

Son: Not really. You know I spend most of my time with N——.

Dad: That must make it hard to keep track of what's going on elsewhere?

Son: I guess I am a little bit out of touch.

Dad: Would you say it's possible that you've lost touch with some of the good things about the world, about people?

Son: You mean that I've developed this pessimistic attitude without really checking it out?

Dad: Yes.

Son: (Pensive) Well, I think that might be true.

Comment: In the preceding dialogue the son starts out with a broadly generalized, completely negative view towards the non-cult world. In response, the father (1) confirms that yes, there are unpleasant aspects to non-cult life; (2) relates, but doesn't dwell on, his own positive experiences; (3) encourages the son to speak in more personal terms; and (4) helps the son reassess his negative world view.

Note that a number of opportunities arise for the father to criticize, debate, or lecture his son. For example, when the son complains about materialistic tendencies, the father could have pointed out that his son's guru lives in luxury. Or, when the son questions the validity of charitable organizations the father could have argued that N—— doesn't provide members with a financial statement. Instead, the father chooses to maintain rapport and let his son arrive at his own conclusions.

By the end of the dialogue, the son is willing to question the validity of his own negative views, an important step in reassessing cult-induced repulsion.

Practical Experience as a Means of Countering Cult-Induced Repulsion

One reason cult members are susceptible to the notion of an evil outside world is that they seldom have opportunities for reality testing. In some cults, members rarely travel beyond the physical confines of the group. In others, members may venture out in pairs or in groups, clinging together for protection against worldly "distractions" and "hostilities." However, even those cultists who have daily contact with the outside world are likely to perceive it as a forbidding place, for they are so sure that people are unhappy, angry, restless, hateful, and the like, that they fail to notice anything (such as a kind gesture) that contradicts their beliefs. Though not physically restricted, these members are psychologically hindered from perceiving the world realistically.

Shared parent-child excursions into the outside world can help counter the effects of cult-imposed repulsion. Exposure to such ordinary occurrences as a couple walking hand-in-hand, a mother strolling her child, or a bus driver helping a disabled man may, in itself, pose a challenge to the cult's negative world view. It is not uncommon, however, for cult members to be out in the world and yet remain oblivious to their surroundings. In such cases, parents can gently point out some of the nice things that are going on (for example, "I think it was very kind of that young man to give his seat to that older woman"). However, parents should avoid forced, overenthusiastic raving about the world (saying, for example, "Isn't this world magnificent/wondrous/splendid?"), for such grand depictions are likely to turn off cult members — and non-cult members, for that matter! — and besides, they simply aren't true. In fact, any excursion into the world is likely to include a number of unpleasant experiences (such as experiencing impatience and rudeness or seeing poor and homeless people). On these occasions, parents can help a child by modeling an appropriate response (for example, by offering an amicable comment to someone who is upset about waiting in a long line).

Afterwards, these shared worldly experiences — both the negative and the positive — can be discussed and evaluated, with parents asking questions to promote critical thinking about the non-cult world (for example, "What did you think of our excursion? Was it what you expected?" Were there especially nice aspects? Upsetting aspects?"

As a child accumulates personal experience with the outside world and begins to evaluate that experience from a critical perspective, he will be better equipped to address questions which call for a realistic comparison, and eventually the choice, between the cult and the non-cult world. For example, parents could ask: "Is the group's view of the world realistic? If not, what is the world really like (from your experience)? What are people [non-cult members] really like? What is it like to live outside the cult? Have you considered asking people you know whether they are really miserable? Is it possible that people who aren't part of the group are good? Happy? Contributing to the world?"

We will address these questions, and others, in Chapter Ten, which deals with Making a Choice. However, it should be noted that the task of critically evaluating the world does not end after a choice has been made. Rather, it is an ongoing task, crucial, of course, to reevaluating the cult, but also crucial to the autonomy we are hoping to promote through this reevaluation process.

One final note on repulsion. Cultists may, on occasion, describe the world in glowing general terms, for example, "This world is precious, and everything in it is sacred." Quite often such statements, rather than expressing a sincere attraction to the non-cult world, are a euphemism for, "The cult world is precious, and everything in it was created by Guru; therefore, everything is sacred." To discern the actual meaning behind the words, parents can (1) become familiar with cult language and (2) encourage their child to use more specific and personal terms.

Non-Cult-Related Anxieties

No one's life is trouble-free. Thus, it is not surprising that people entering cults bring certain problems, anxieties, and fears with them into the group. These non-cult-related anxieties may include family conflicts, social, academic, or vocational fears, disillusionment with society, physical or psychological problems, and the like. As noted earlier, cults routinely exaggerate, exacerbate, or otherwise exploit such conflicts as a means of attracting and maintaining members (for example, by convincing recruits that they never had a good relationship with their parents, and then promising an ideal family within the cult).

Actually, members' pre-cult anxieties, suppressed by a physically demanding lifestyle and mind-control techniques, often seem to disappear during their cult years. However, these anxieties commonly resurface, unresolved, during the process of voluntary reevaluation, causing strong resistance to leaving the cult and returning to the outside world.

A number of steps can be taken to help lessen non-cult-related anxieties, including anticipating potential anxieties, promoting discussions which address these anxieties, and providing practical experiences which encourage reality-testing and problem-solving.

Anticipating Potential Anxieties
Parents can anticipate the particular issues which may be troubling their child by reviewing her pre-cult history and listening for relevant remarks.

Pre-Cult History
The following questions are intended to help pinpoint pre-cult problem areas. In considering the questions, parents should try to recall and write down specific details.

Before entering the cult:
- Was your son/daughter troubled by family problems? Specifics?

- Did your son/daughter express or display academic anxiety or failure, or confusion over what to study? Specifics?
- Did your son/daughter express or display career-related anxiety, confusion, or failure? Specifics?
- Was your son/daughter afflicted by physical ailments or disabilities, or related fears? Specifics?
- Did your son/daughter engage in destructive habits (such as drug or alcohol abuse, smoking, overeating)? Specifics?
- Did your son/daughter experience periods of psychological distress (such as depression, sharp mood swings, suicidal tendencies)? Specifics?
- Did your son/daughter have problems with social skills (such as developing casual and/or intimate relationships, and dating)? Specifics?
- Did your son/daughter have problems with self-image? Specifics?
- Did your son/daughter express or display religious or spiritual frustrations (such as disillusionment with family religion)? Specifics?
- Was your son/daughter disillusioned with society? Specifics?
- Was your son/daughter particularly troubled by a situational stress (caused by the death of a relative or friend, failure of an intimate relationship, or the like)? Specifics?
- Was your son/daughter anxious about becoming an autonomous adult (and, therefore, emotionally, financially, and domestically self-supporting)? Specifics?

Answering the above questions will help sensitize parents to *potentially* troubling non-cult issues. To determine the actual relevance of these issues, and whether or not they are cult-related, parents should listen for pertinent comments and then engage their son or daughter in exploratory discussion.

Recognizing Relevant Comments
The following are examples of comments which may indicate that a cultist feels anxious over non-cult-related issues:

- "You know, Dad and I never really got along." (May indicate anxiety over pre-cult relationship with father; *or*, reflect cult-induced estrangement from parents.)
- "I probably wouldn't have been a good lawyer, anyway." (May indicate career anxieties, *or*, regret over having to give up her career after joining the cult.)
- "I could not imagine being a parent." (May indicate pre-cult anxiety about marriage and children; *or*, reflect cult-induced distaste for parenthood.)
- "I don't think I'm a student by nature." (May indicate pre-cult academic anxiety; *or*, reflect cult's negative attitude toward schooling.)

Through discussion with their child, parents can gain a better understanding about pre-cult and cult-induced anxieties.

Discussions about pre-cult anxieties can help a cultist (1) articulate her concerns, (2) reality test (for example, are her concerns grounded in fact?), (3) alleviate some of her anxieties, and (4) rediscover her own problem-solving abilities.

Sample Dialogue: Non-Cult-Related Anxieties:

Daughter: You know, Dad and I don't really get along. I don't feel like we're friends.

Mother: You wish your relationship with him was different?

Daughter: Well, yes. I've been thinking about this a lot. It seems like whenever I try to talk to him, he ends up lecturing me, and then I don't feel like talking anymore.

Mother: It seems as though he's not really listening to you?

Daughter: Exactly! And he's been doing that to me ever since I was a child. (Pauses) I don't think it's ever going to change, either.

Mother: You feel like giving up?

Daughter: Yes, because it seems so futile. (Pause) But on the other hand, he *is* my father. I just don't know what to do.

Mother: It sounds as if you'd like to be close with him, if you knew it was possible?

Daughter: I guess that's true. I really care about him. (Pause) And I guess he cares about me, too. What do you think?

Mother: I think he loves you very much.

Daughter: But what about the way we get along, or don't get along?

Mother: Well, let me ask you this: do you think your relationship with him is all bad?

Daughter: (Pauses to reflect) No, not always. We've had some close moments, like that time he rushed me to the hospital for that appendix operation. But most of the time it isn't good. It seems that whenever I do something he doesn't like, he has to make that the focus of every conversation, no matter what I want to talk about. For example, ten years ago, when I took chemistry instead of French, he was furious. Night and day he tried to convince me I was wrong. He couldn't talk about anything else. And the same thing used to happen when I dated somebody he didn't like. And now, I am constantly being lectured and criticized for belonging to N—— (cult name). Do you understand what I'm saying, or do you think I'm crazy?

Mother: I think you're being realistic and mature, facing the fact that there is a problem. I know that the two of you often have trouble talking to each other without getting angry. But I think there's hope.

Daughter: You actually think he could change?

Mother: I think it wouldn't be easy, but that together the two of you could work something out. I think both of you have the strength to change.

Daughter: (Surprised) Both of us change? (Pause) You know, maybe you're right. Maybe part of it is my fault. Maybe even most of it. I try to be loving, but I guess I'm not loving enough. I know I should pray more. I feel like a failure. (Falls back into cult interpretations, in this case that prayer will make everything perfect, and if things go wrong it is because the member isn't trying hard enough.)

Mother: (Gently) I don't agree with you there. I don't think either one of you is to blame.

Daughter: Then what did you mean when you said both of us had to change?

Mother: I said you both had the strength to change. And I meant that both you and your father are strong people. When you set your mind to accomplish something, you usually succeed.

Daughter: Like that time Dad managed to keep his job even though his boss was intent on firing him?

Mother: Yes. And do you remember the year you had a math teacher you hated?

Daughter: (Laughing) Oh God, yes. His only problem was that he didn't know how to teach math. I remember I had to buy three extra books that year and teach myself!

Mother: And you got an A in the course.

Daughter: What an experience. I'll never forget that. (Pauses) So, what you were trying to say before was that if Dad and I set our minds to getting along better, we could probably do it?

Mother: Yes, what do you think?

Daughter: I'm not sure, but I think there might be some hope.

Comment. In this dialogue, the daughter introduces an issue, her relationship with her father, which seems to indicate non-cult-related anxiety. In response, the mother:

- Asks questions based on her daughter's remarks, to encourage her daughter to clarify and express her thoughts and feelings more fully, by saying, for example: "You wish your relationship with him was different? It seems as if he's not really listening to you? You feel like giving up?" You'd like to be close, if you knew it was possible?"
- Offers her opinion as a means of showing support: "I think he loves you very much; I think you're being realistic and mature; I think there's hope; I think that it wouldn't be easy, but that together the two of you could work something out."
- Encourages her daughter to evaluate the situation critically: "Do you think your relationship with him is all bad?"
- When asked, confirms the existence of a problem: "I think... there is a problem."
- Gently disagrees when her daughter lapses into cult rhetoric about not praying enough.
- Reminds her daughter of her strengths, both general ("When you set your mind to accomplish something, you usually succeed.") and specific (by noting the math teacher incident).
- At the end, reflects back to her daughter the question of whether or not to try to resolve the problem.

Note: Even though the daughter cites her cult membership as one of the problem areas in her relationship with her father ("I am constantly being lectured and criticized for belonging to N——."), the communication difficulties in this parent-child relationship seem to have started before the daughter's cult involvement. Therefore, we assume that the cult is not at the root of the problem (though it may exacerbate it), and classify this as a non-cult-related anxiety.

By the end of the dialogue the daughter feels more hopeful about working towards an improved relationship with her father. At this point, mother and daughter could begin to discuss and evaluate practical strategies for addressing the problem. Of course, Dad's cooperation will be necessary.

Practical Strategies

It is unrealistic to expect a child to resolve all or even most of her non-cult anxieties while she is still reevaluating the cult. Therefore, we recommend setting priorities to determine which non-cult anxieties should be addressed right away, and which should be left until after the reevaluation task has been completed. The following are general guidelines for setting priorities. However, we urge parents to study their particular situations to determine what seems best for their son or daughter.

- Non-cult-related anxieties which, if addressed, are likely to confuse, complicate, or otherwise impede the reevaluation process, should be put on hold until later.
- Non-cult-related anxieties which, if ignored, are likely to interfere with the reevaluation process, should be attended to right away. For example, family conflicts such as the father-daughter relationship in the preceding dialogue are important to attend to, for if a child is thinking about leaving a cult, it may help to know she can turn to her family for support.

In some cases, non-cult anxieties can be addressed directly; parents and child can plan a strategy for gently entering into feared situations. For example, the daughter in the preceding dialogue could further discuss her concerns with her mother, anticipate and role-play a father-daughter conversation which addresses the problems in their relationship, and write down her specific hopes, fears, goals, and even some of the things she wants to say to her father. Then, when she feels ready, she could talk directly to her father about their relationship.

In other cases, counseling may be a more constructive route (if, for example, the father and daughter are unable to work things out with each other). If a son or daughter is willing to enter counseling, we advise parents to seek a cult-aware professional, for although the initial reason for counseling may be non-cult-related, cult issues are bound to arise in the course of therapy.

Attractions to the Non-Cult World

Parents often become so preoccupied with the cult's manipulations of their child and the consequent family alienation that they forget or grossly underestimate the extent to which their child is bonded, so to speak, to people and events in the non-cult world. As noted earlier, cults will often work systematically to neutralize these attachments. But they rarely destroy them completely; the attachments continue to exist in the cultist's mind, however suppressed they may be.

The parents' goals with regard to this factor are twofold: (1) to identify that which their child formerly (and/or currently) found (finds) attractive about the non-cult world, and (2) to work systematically to "unsuppress" and strengthen these attractions.

Identifying the non-cult attractions is usually a simple task, for family members know each other intimately. These attractions tend to fall under the following categories:

- relationships with (extended) family members;
- relationships with friends;
- academic goals;
- vocational goals;
- leisure activities — intellectual, athletic, social, musical, artistic, etc.

The first step in strengthening these attractions to the non-cult world is simply to develop a mindset to remind the cultist of these things when she is communicating with parents. We often recommend, for example, that parents, when writing or talking to a cult-involved child, relate news that would be of interest to the child they knew before the cult intervened. Examples:

- cousin Laura's new baby boy;
- a trade between the Redlegs and the Giants;
- a moving play you recently attended;
- a friend's taking a job with a law firm;

It can also be helpful to mobilize friends and family members. Ask other persons the cult-involved child cares about to write, call, visit him, or invite him to visit.

Lastly, when your child shows some interest in the non-cult world, encourage it. If she asks about Aunt Hannah, tell her that Aunt Hannah says she misses her, that Aunt Hannah is coming for dinner next month and would be delighted if she (the cultist) came, or whatever is appropriate.

The point is to remember that your child still has in his mind, however buried, a multitude of attachments and interests not aimed at the cult. Use your imagination to awaken these attachments and interests.

Cults: What Parents Should Know   *109*

Keep in mind, however, that the cult's influence may prevent your child from demonstrating his past level of interest (or even any interest) in your communications. Try not to let your emotions get the best of you in these situations. You must function somewhat like a psychotherapist respecting the defenses of a client who can't bear to face certain truths. Be patient. Let your statements register in his mind. Even if he shows no interest, the communication may affect him on an unconscious or private level. Plant seeds. Don't be pushy and overdo your news reports. But don't give up, either.

Chapter Ten

Towards Making a Choice

The thrust of this entire reevaluation process has been to stimulate a cultist's critical thinking about the cult and the non-cult world, in preparation for making an informed choice between the two. However, one peculiar effect of destructive cultism is that members often remain loyal despite clear evidence that the group and/or the leader are manipulative, unethical, and harmful to members and to society. This irrational loyalty is a common source of confusion and frustration to parents, who can't understand why their child "won't face the facts."

In our counseling work we have found that in most cases the cultist is not being obstinate, but rather that the idea of leaving the cult simply hasn't occurred to him. Often, he still believes cult practices lie outside the realm of human judgment. Thus, the task of introducing the idea of leaving and promoting a choice often falls upon the shoulders of the parents. "But at what point," a parent might ask, "will my child be ready to choose?"

The following are general guidelines to help determine when and how to help a cult member make this crucial decision. If appropriate and feasible, outside resources such as professionals and ex-cult members should be included in this process. Again, we urge parents to use their discretion in determining the timing and approach that best suits their situation.

Evaluating the Consequences of Cult Influences

Cult Manipulation

When? When a son or daughter recognizes and can talk about the group's use of unethical manipulation (for example, deceit, group pressure, information control, isolation, mind-control) in recruitment, solicitation, and keeping members loyal.

How? Parents can ask their child to consider questions like: If the group is deceptive, what does that tell me about the group? About the leader? How do I feel about the use of deception? Can I trust a group that manipulates me? That encourages me to manipulate others? Do I want to participate in these kinds of activities? According to my own values, is this type of behavior right or wrong, good or bad?

Cult Repulsion

When? When a son or daughter recognizes and can talk about aspects of the group which are unpleasant, unhealthy, or otherwise upsetting (such as overworking, lack of privacy, regimented lifestyle, poor nutrition, hostility towards outsiders, denial of personal desires for career, marriage, education, children, corruption among the leadership).

How? Parents can ask their child to consider: Do I want to subject myself to these unpleasant/unhealthy/upsetting conditions? If the group and leader advocate an unhealthy lifestyle, what does that say about their attitude toward members? Does the group care what happens to me? Does the leader care? If not, can I trust them? Do I want to devote myself to people who aren't concerned about me? Do I want to put myself in their hands? What other options do I have?

Cult Attractions

When? When a son or daughter recognizes and talks about cult attractions from a critical perspective (saying, for example, "Many of the things that attracted me to this group in the first place aren't true; membership isn't free; the group isn't working to help the poor, the hungry, the disabled; it isn't promoting world peace; I am not happier or more loving now than before I joined; I haven't gained total control over my life; the leader doesn't practice what he preaches; the members aren't one happy family — they fight among themselves just like people outside the group."

How? Parents can ask their child to consider: What was I looking for and hoping for when I joined this group? Am I getting what I expected? If not, why? Is it my own fault? Or is it possible that the group doesn't really offer what it promises? If the group makes false promises, what does that tell me? Do I want to affiliate with, support, and be a representative of such a group? Which attractions are real? What benefits have I reaped (a sense of purpose, leadership skills, moments of ecstasy)? Are the benefits worth the price? Can I get the benefits elsewhere?

Overall Evaluation of the Cult

When? After the specific areas of cult manipulation, repulsion, and attraction have been sufficiently evaluated.

How? Parents can ask their child to consider: In light of what I know about the group and the leader, what is my overall evaluation? Is membership in the group beneficial to me, to others, to society? In what ways? Is membership in the group harmful to me, to others, to society? In what ways? Are the group's/leader's attitude and practices ethical towards me, towards others, towards society? How? Unethical? How? Is my membership worth the price?

Considering the Possibility of Reentering Society

Cult-Induced Repulsion Towards the Outside World

When? When a cultist recognizes that (1) he's been out of touch with the outside world; (2) his perceptions of the world are inaccurate and overly negative; (3) through discussion, reading, and practical experience, he's discovered that the world is a more attractive place than he'd thought, with both good and bad elements.

How? Parents can ask their child to consider: Am I being fair to myself by remaining cut off from the outside world? Since my perceptions seem to have been inaccurate, don't I owe it to myself to find out the truth? Don't I want to know what the outside world is really like? (Parents might suggest that their child spend more time gaining practical experience, and possibly encourage a commitment to spend 2-6 months either at home or with trusted cult-aware relatives or friends.) Do I really know what people are like outside the group? What is the quality of their lives? (Parents can encourage ongoing contact and development of relationships with people outside the cult.) Are there activities, hopes, dreams, goals I would like to pursue outside the group? (Parents can encourage their child to articulate personal desires.) What don't I like about the outside world? Can I live with, overcome, or work to change some of these troubling factors? (Parents can encourage their child to articulate his negative feelings about the world, and either model or discuss ways of dealing with these feelings.)

Non-Cult-Related Anxieties

When? When a cultist can say, "There are aspects of my pre-group life that still bother me, and I feel it's important for me to start resolving these issues."

How? Parents can suggest and help link a child up with non-cult resources for addressing these anxieties (for example, counseling). While this response doesn't directly promote a choice, it helps establish an outside support system to which the cultist can turn upon leaving the cult. It also may tip the balance of forces toward leaving the cult.

Choosing Between Worlds

Choosing between the cult and the non-cult world is the final task in the process of voluntary reevaluation. This entails (1) recognizing the necessity of a choice and (2) developing a strategy for making that choice.

Attractions

When? When a cultist shows even indirect interest in aspects of the non-cult world.

How? Talk about that which seems to interest your child. Use your imagination to connect her to other persons who may help strengthen these interests.

Mutually Exclusive Worlds

When criticized for their isolationist doctrines and practices, destructive cults often retort that their members spend a good deal of time participating in mainstream society. At first glance this appears true, as one does find cultists who are full-time students, others working at full-time jobs outside the group, still others living in private (rather than communal cult) dwellings, and even some who manage their own financial affairs.

Yet upon closer inspection, one discovers that the committed cultist, though he may be physically accessible, is psychologically estranged from society. He has accepted, often unconsciously, the cult construct of an artificial dichotomy dividing the world into two mutually exclusive "worlds": (1) the cult and (2) the outside world. And in pledging allegiance to the cult, he has — again, often unwittingly — excluded himself from "membership" in mainstream society.

To help a cultist recognize this mutual exclusivity, and the ensuing inevitability of a choice, parents can ask their child to consider: How does my membership in the group affect my relationship with the rest of the world? And, more specifically:

- According to the group's ideals, how much of my life (that is, time, money, loyalty) should I devote to the group? How much of my life should I devote to non-group activities, interests, causes?

- According to group ideals, how much responsibility should I feel towards my job? If the leader asks me to take time off, should I comply? If he asks me to quit, should I comply?

- According to group ideals, how much responsibility should I feel to obey the laws of the land? If the leader asks me to do something unlawful, am I supposed to comply? To what extent? Lie? Steal? Destroy property? Murder?

- According to group ideals, how much responsibility should I assume for the welfare of non-members? For my family? If I were asked to choose between helping a group member or helping my family, what would the group expect of me?

• According to group doctrine, what should my appraisal be of the outside world? Good or evil? An illusion? A distraction from the truth? A temptation-ground for material desires and carnal lust? A jungle of ignorance and spiritual decay?

• According to group ideals, how should I interact with the outside world? As a full participant? As an aloof observer? Avoid all unnecessary contact?

• According to group ideals, should I consider myself a member of both worlds? If not, doesn't that necessitate a choice?

Suggestions for Promoting an Informed Choice

Even after recognizing the inevitability of a choice, cultists are often beset with the dilemma, "How do I make the choice?" The following suggestions reflect ideas we have found useful in our work with cultists who are trying to make this decision. These can be readily adopted by parents:

• Suggest viewing the choice as a problem to be solved.
• Discuss and write down ideas regarding what constitutes a constructive problem-solving attitude (patience, willingness to learn, willingness to change, for example). Also, encourage the cultist to express her opinion.
• Help the cultist define the problem clearly.
• Help the cultist plan and implement a practical strategy. This strategy should include:
  - Collecting, consolidating, reviewing, and analyzing the following information: personal thoughts, feelings, and experiences with the cult; books and articles (pro and con) about the cult; "members only" and public cult literature (*We strongly recommend studying this literature with former members and non-members; alone, the cultist is apt to become confused, deceived, or persuaded by the lulling familiarity of cult jargon and logic.*); general information on cults, persuasion, hypnosis, brainwashing, mind-control, and other related subjects.
  - Seeking opinions, experiences, and support from others: former members, cult-aware professionals, family; pre-cult friends, advisors, teachers, counselors. (Cultists may need extra encouragement in this area, since suspicion of non-members is a prominent attitude in destructive cults. Parents can remind their child that listening to others does not constitute acquiescence, and that the child is free to use or discard the ideas of others in coming to her own conclusions.)
  - Anticipating the consequences of staying in or leaving the cult, and of remaining apart from or returning to the non-cult world. The following

are questions for the cultist to consider in evaluating the potential consequences of her choice:

What are the potential benefits of staying in the group? What have I gained? (Benefits may include: freedom from worldly responsibilities; continued association with group members, sense of identity as a committed member, freedom from ambiguity and uncertainty, devotion to a living guru, elitist status, refuge from loneliness, independence from parents, freedom from parental expectations, sense of pride in honoring one's commitment, etc.)

What are the potential losses/risks/harms of staying in the group? While many cults expect a lifetime commitment, they often don't give members a chance to think through the consequences of remaining in the group for their entire lives. It is one thing to forego sexual relations, marriage, parenthood, career, and education from day to day; it is another, much more severe consideration, to abstain from sex *forever*, to *never* get married or have children, etc.

Parents can help a child recognize the negative consequences of staying in the cult by encouraging him to think about his long-term future with questions like: What would it be like to stay in the group for my entire life? To grow old there? To maintain the cult-prescribed lifestyle, beliefs, and practices as long as I'm alive? (Losses and harms may include: unfulfilled personal desires, strained or severed ties with non-cult members, wasted talents and skills, denial of sexuality, relinquished autonomy, suppressed individuality and critical faculties, exhaustion and ill health, etc.)

What are the potential benefits of leaving the group? Which aspects of the group would I like to get away from? (for example, restrictive lifestyle, diet, corruption, dislike of members).

What are the potential benefits of returning to mainstream society? What have I missed about the outside world? More specifically, are there activities I've missed while in the group? (Parents can remind the cultist of activities she found pleasurable in the past.) Are there people I've missed spending time with? (Parents can provide reminders.) Are there relationships I've wanted to pursue but felt restricted from pursuing as a group member? What hopes, dreams, goals have I given up while in the group? (This particular question is strange for cultists, who have lived under the cult-imposed assumption that personal goals are "selfish," egotistical, unspiritual, meaningless, even evil. Parents can help by reminding their child of the goals she had before entering the group.) Do I have new hopes, dreams, goals I'd like to pursue?

(*Comment*: These questions are intended to help a cultist recognize that there are potentially positive aspects of returning to mainstream society. However, *the major work of defining and pursuing specific personal goals is often best left until a cultist decides to leave the cult.*)

What are the potential losses involved in leaving the group? What things might I miss if I left? (for example, cult friends; simplistic lifestyle that precludes decision-making; other aspects of the group which are attractive). How might I compensate for these losses should I leave?

What harms might I face if I leave? What does the group say will happen to defectors? (for example, that they will go insane, become contemptible persons, be punished by God, live a meaningless existence, see their parents, relatives and friends punished). Which, if any, of these consequences are realistic? Do I know people who have left the group? Are they suffering these consequences? Would it help to talk with them about the actual harms of defecting?

What problems might I face in returning to mainstream society? This question is intended to help identify and articulate the potential conflicts of reentry. However, *the actual task of facing and resolving these conflicts is best left until after a cultist decides to leave the cult.* Potential conflicts may include: harassment by cult, absence of purpose, loneliness, awkwardness, estrangement, confusion, questions, ambiguities, uncertainties (for example: "What is the meaning of life? How can I distinguish between right and wrong? Where will I live? How will I support myself? How can I catch up on the developmental skills appropriate for people my age?") Since many of these questions can seem overwhelming, parents may need to help their child focus on taking one step at a time, encouraging him to concentrate first on his reevaluation of the cult, and later on the problems of reentry.

Accepting Responsibility for Choosing

It is not uncommon for cultists on the threshold of making a decision to panic at the thought, "What if I make the wrong choice?" Parents can anticipate and minimize this panic by helping their child recognize that: (1) part of being human is to make mistakes; (2) you can only decide on the basis of what you know; (3) as an autonomous adult, you are *responsible* to act upon what you know; and (4) the decision is not irreversible. If, at a later date, you feel you have made the wrong choice, you can always change your mind.

Responding to a Child's Choice

If, after completing the task of voluntary reevaluation, a cultist decides to stay with the group, parents are advised to keep communication lines open and remind the child that she is free to change her mind. This can be a very upsetting moment for parents, but we strongly suggest they refrain from making important changes in strategy until they have time to reflect upon and reevaluate their situation; many ex-cultists returned to their cults at least once before leaving for good.

If a cultist decides to leave the group, parents should be prepared to help him face the challenge of reentry.

Chapter Eleven

The Challenge of Reentry

Post-Cult Sunrise
By Joan Carol Ross

Where have I been? In a dream? A delirium?
Was that a war I fought, with cause just and fair,
or simply a frenzied march to implement his whim?
And those who marched beside, chanting, praising, believing,
were they friends or faces?
Was it substance or mist I held precious?
And he who held the baton, shall he be avenged or forgotten?

Here I am now, but where is this?
Have I been ill, perhaps died and returned?
I try, I try, to glean form and meaning,
but all that moves seems indifferent to my awkward presence.

What language shall I speak? Mother, father,
how do I embrace you? I don't know.
How do I receive your embrace? I don't know.
My arms are rigid; my heart, hollow; my words, clumsy;
my head, besieged.

To whom can I turn? The mirror laughs or scolds,
reflecting someone else.
The family peers into my invisible cage.
The ocean renders some comfort in her rhythm and froth.
But whence comes her salt? Is there God or none?
Who am I? An incomplete resumé? An anachronistic poem?
Will yesterday's clothes bring back the words and feelings
I seem to have lost?

Tomorrow, tomorrow. What time shall I awaken?
What is the Plan? Eat and sleep? Eat and sleep.
And question the Why and How and When.
And whither?

Don't ask me questions. I'm not prepared.
Please don't come too close, don't touch me yet.
I cannot defend.
And yet, if I could hope,
I would ask you to ask me all about that Time:
when I fought valiantly to preserve a dream;
when I did my best to ripen into a sweet fruit;
when I toiled to pave a smooth road towards peace,
along which we might have walked together.
And if I could trust, I might ask you to help me:
to tell me how it's done —
how, for instance, to wake up with a purpose;
how to manage the interminable minutes between now and then;
how to embrace the tasks before me with confidence;
how to dare to hope for better tomorrows;
how to make a friend,
and how to be a friend.

What is it like to leave a cult and reenter the outside world? As the poem above suggests, the transition is awkward and painful, laden with questions and uncertainties. Some have compared it to being released from prison, getting discharged from a hospital, or returning home from a war.

In our counseling work we have found that relief, exhilaration, freedom, hope, power, and reunion with family and friends are often part of the recent ex-cultist's experience. So too are confusion, depression, indecisiveness, loneliness, anger, guilt, disillusionment, and shame. In short, reentry is a complex process that requires much time and effort and patience on the part of both former cultists and their parents. While the experience is different for each family, we have outlined below some of the common problems, needs, and tasks associated with reentry. In doing so, we hope to help parents anticipate and deal with the particular stresses that accompany this period of transition.

Common Problems
Depression. Recent ex-cultists often have trouble getting out of bed in the morning; during the day they may be reluctant to go out or even to socialize with people at home; at night they may find it difficult to fall asleep. These symptoms, which may continue for weeks, months, occasionally even years, often reflect feelings of loss and mourning. First, there is the immediate loss of that which the cult may have provided: companionship, prestige, sense of identity and direction, and sense of purpose. Second, there is the loss of time spent in the cult which might have been better spent in other ways (enjoying one's family, getting married, childbearing and child rearing, accumulating experiences parallel to one's peers, and dating) which promote social and

psychological development, and pursuing educational and career goals. Third, former cultists must contend with a loss of innocence, acknowledging their participation in the cult world of exploitation and deceit, and recognizing their vulnerability to psychological coercion.

Parents can help by encouraging (even initiating) discussion about these losses; showing sympathy and understanding; and helping the ex-cultist focus on some of the gains made (for example, skills acquired) during the cult years.

Guilt. Ex-cultists often feel guilty for having recruited people into the cult, for leaving cult friends behind, and for having neglected their family and friends while in the cult.

Parents can help by telling their child that they understand that much of her behavior was largely a result of cult conditioning, and that they forgive her. If guilt feelings are intense and intractable, professional counseling should be considered.

Loneliness. People leaving cults often feel terribly isolated because (1) they are unaccustomed to trusting "outsiders"; (2) they don't trust their own thoughts, perceptions, and feelings; (3) people treat them as though they had just returned from the dead; and (4) because they "burned bridges" when they joined the cult, they may no longer have close non-cult friends.

Parents can help by acknowledging the loneliness and gently encouraging participation in low-key social activities (such as meals with family and friends), gradually encouraging greater levels of participation.

Indecisiveness. Since cults often teach total reliance on the leader, former cultists commonly find it difficult to make decisions.

Parents can help by providing opportunities for shared decision-making, remaining patient while the former member is trying to make up his mind, allowing him to change his mind and make mistakes, gradually increasing his responsibility for making decisions.

Poor judgment. Again because they are out of practice, ex-cultists may show poor judgment in their choice of friends, lifestyle, or activities.

Parents can help by allowing their child to make mistakes, by modeling more appropriate behavior, discussing their concerns directly with their child, and, in cases where the behavior is truly destructive (as in excessive drinking), gently suggesting that the child seek outside help (such as counseling).

Floating. Ex-cultists sometimes slip — involuntarily — into a cult frame of mind similar to the trance-like state they sometimes experienced in the cult. Called "floating," this altered state can be triggered by stress, depression, or significant words, songs, or ideas associated with the cult. When they are floating, ex-members often feel as though they never left the cult; afterwards, many wonder which of the "two selves" is real. This fluctuation can be very disconcerting.

Parents can help by: explaining the floating phenomenon to their child so that she can anticipate it and be less upset by it; staying alert for cult-like (floating) behavior (such as the use of cult words and tone of voice "spaciness"); and helping her out of the floating state by focusing on concrete (rather than abstract) topics. *Note*: Although we advise parents to be observant, being overly vigilant about floating can make an ex-cultist feel worse. The ideal is to prepare the former member so she can deal with the problem herself, for example, by helping her identify and avoid the particular activities that seem to trigger floating episodes.

Reductionist, simplistic thinking. Upon leaving the cult, former members often find it oppressive to think in anything but simplistic terms. Thus, people, things, events, and ideas are either good or bad, right or wrong, with no shades of gray. There is very little tolerance of ambiguity or complexity of thought. However, most ex-cultists regain former levels of mental competence with increased time away from the cult.

Parents can help by being patient, modeling mature thinking processes, and stimulating their child by asking questions that require him to make distinctions and acknowledge ambiguities.

Fear of retribution. Responding to cult threats about defection, former cultists often fear harassment or harm when they leave the group.

Parents can help by encouraging discussion regarding these fears and helping the child sort out which, if any, are likely to be realized. If there does seem to be danger of cult retaliation, parents might consider changing their telephone number or contacting appropriate law-enforcement authorities. In most cases, however, cults will turn their attention to recruiting new members rather than spending time (and money) trying to retrieve defectors.

Spiritual, philosophical, or ideological void. Having lived within the absolutist ideology of a cult, former members often experience a spiritual-philosophical emptiness when they leave. Many were puzzled, dissatisfied, or actively searching for spiritual meaning before the cult, and in fact may have joined with the hope that the group would satisfy their yearnings. How terribly disappointing, then, to leave the cult and find themselves still searching, possibly even more confused than before, without a reliable base from which to interpret or understand the world. This absence of a spiritual-philosophical framework can be very disturbing, sometimes prompting ex-members to reach out for a substitute ideology.

Parents can help by : suggesting that the former member wait a few months and gain some distance from the cult before trying to resolve spiritual-philosophical issues; reassuring him that in due time he will develop his own philosophy, morality, and spirituality; letting him know that it's "normal" to feel in conflict over such issues; acknowledging his loss of security in giving up the cult ideology; helping him address such questions as, "Is there a God? Is there a way to satisfy my spiritual needs? Do I want to go back to my former religion?", thus openly discussing the danger in seeking a substitute ideology (which might lead him unwittingly to enter into a cult-like situation); and referring him to knowledgeable clergy.

Parent-child antagonism. Ex-cultists may balk at the idea of moving back home with their parents, often because they fear their parents will treat them as children. Ironically, one of the most common parental fears centers on the responsibility/burden of taking care of a grown-up child. These tensions frequently erupt in the form of parent-child antagonism. For example: ex-cultists may get angry with their parents for pushing them too fast, for overprotecting them, or for not being understanding enough. And parents often become impatient with their child's seemingly slow progress, lethargy, "laziness," or depression.

Parents can help by having frank, caring discussions to alleviate the tension and enable the family to work cooperatively. However, if the strain persists (and this may be due to non-cult-related family problems), it could result in a destructive pattern, in which case we advise parents to seek family counseling (with the ex-cultist, if she's willing). Alternatively, the ex-cultist might seek individual counseling. The point is, a supportive, but not a smothering, family relationship is important to a former member's successful reentry into mainstream society.

Difficulty communicating. Former cultists need an outlet to express the intense thoughts and emotions that accompany reentry. However, having grown accustomed to the cult "tongue," ex-members often have trouble articulating their own thoughts and feelings in direct, personal terms. This can be extremely frustrating.

Parents can help by showing patience, encouraging their child to speak in personal terms (rather than generalities), and modeling good communication skills (generally, the more exposure an ex-cultist has to normal language, the more articulate he'll become).

Common Needs

Privacy. Former cultists often demand a lot of privacy (this is especially true where the cult living conditions were crowded). If at all possible, ex-members should be given space, such as a private bedroom, where they can close the door and be alone with their thoughts, hopes, and fears.

Medical attention. We recommend a medical checkup even for those whose lifestyle was moderately healthy while in the cult, and especially in cases where the cultist worked long hours with little rest, poor nutrition, and/or in crowded and unsanitary living conditions.

Lifestyle

Daily routine: If daily life in the cult was rigidly controlled, former members may feel the need to experiment with different time schedules and activities. For example, they may want to sleep late in the mornings or stay up late at night. *Or*, they might be reluctant to plan in advance because they feel it will confine them or rob them of free time. *Or*, they may be uncomfortable with free time and want help in structuring their days. Parents should be sensitive to their child's desires/needs regarding time management, and should offer emotional support and constructive criticism as he experiments.

Diet. If diet was prescribed in the cult, ex-members may want to try out different foods. *Or*, they may prefer to retain the diet they had in the cult (such as vegetarianism). Although this may be inconvenient for parents, ex-members should be allowed to choose their own diets, as long as they are getting adequate nutrition. If parents feel burdened by the prospect of preparing separate meals, they might consider asking the former member to help out with the food shopping and preparation.

Appearance. If the cult prescribed a particular style of dress and personal appearance, former members may want to experiment with different clothes, hairstyles, makeup, etc., before settling on their own personal style. For example, if members were required to appear clean-cut, an ex-cultist may want to grow a beard and wear jeans. As a general rule, parents should try to show tolerance and understanding, and not insist that their child's appearance reflect their own lifestyle and values. In addition, ex-members often need clothes upon leaving the cult, and parents should try to provide — within their means — an adequate wardrobe for their son or daughter.

Rest and exercise. Sufficient rest and exercise should be a regular part of an ex-cultist's lifestyle, and parents should offer gentle encouragement and role modeling (indeed, they also should get rest and exercise) in this area.

Independence. Ex-cultists returning home feel (and are) very dependent upon their parents. At the same time, they often want and need to feel independent. Parents can help by providing: money (either by giving their child an allowance or the opportunity to earn or borrow money); transportation (for example, allowing the child to use the family car; or driving her where she wants/needs to go; or encouraging her — instructing her if need be — to use public transportation); responsibility (for example, asking the child to participate in household tasks, encouraging her to register to vote, requesting that she assess and keep track of her own financial needs and expenditures); self-sufficiency (for example, as the ex-cultist regains confidence and competence, parents can guide and support her efforts to get a job, achieve financial independence, and move into her own — or a shared — dwelling). The parents' overall goal is to move the child from a dependent to an independent relationship with the parents.

Intellectual stimulation. To help an ex-cultist regain any mental competence lost while in the cult, parents can suggest and share intellectually stimulating activities and materials (based on their child's particular interests, capabilities, and needs). For example, the family could go to a lecture or play; or, the former cultist may be interested in taking a course just for fun.

Social Needs

Confidants. To lessen post-cult loneliness, ex-members need someone to confide in (preferably several people). In the first few months, these confidants are often other ex-members, family, and/or pre-cult friends. Parents should encourage these relationships, and others which seem to fulfill their child's social needs. But do not feel responsible to meet all the child's intimacy needs.

Role models. As noted earlier, cultists are often isolated from or oblivious to the "how-to's" of survival in the non-cult world. Thus, recent ex-members need role models to provide them with clues for successfully managing their lives. Parents will continue to serve as role models. In addition, casual contact with salespeople, waiters, bank tellers, clerks, etc., can also provide examples of appropriate behavior, language, and dress from which ex-cultists can learn. Parents should try to make sure their son or daughter has contact with a variety of role models, and should be willing to discuss these persons with the child.

Professional counseling. While we do recommend counseling (from a cult-aware professional), we recognize that recent ex-members are often very protective of their privacy and understandably reluctant to confide in or seek help from strangers. Thus, parents should suggest (but not insist on) counseling as a potential helping resource to their child. (*Note*: If severe psychological distress is evident, parents should personally consult a mental health professional for advice.)

Common Tasks

The tasks facing former cultists may seem overwhelming at times. They are many, they are varied, and they are difficult. They require time, and patience, and persistence. There will be failures and successes; highs and lows and very-lows; embarrassments; falterings and accomplishments.

But it is not only ex-cultists who must adapt, endure, and overcome. Parents, too, are acutely sensitive to the ups and downs of reentry. They need reassurance, from their child and from outside sources. They need to vent frustrations and fears; to confess feelings of guilt and excitement, to spend time away from their child, to seek support, encouragement, and sometimes professional assistance.

Because parents are so intimately involved in the reentry process, we have listed below, in addition to the ex-cultists' tasks, the tasks that confront parents during this time.

Tasks Facing Ex-Cultists

Rebuild self-trust. In the cult world, "self," "mind," and "ego" are seen as enemies. Thus, recent ex-members must rebuild their respect and confidence in their own thoughts, feelings, and perceptions.

Develop personal morals. Once they shed cult definitions of right and wrong, former members must develop a personal system of morality; they must learn to use their own judgment in resolving ethical and moral issues.

Time management. In many cults, "time is an illusion. The only reality is here and now." Coming from this perspective, recent ex-members need to relearn the value of time; how to use time efficiently and effectively; how to plan ahead; and how to be reliable.

Rebuild social skills:
- learn to participate in casual conversation
- renew and enrich personal vocabulary
- observe and practice appropriate social behavior
- develop ongoing relationships (both casual and intimate)
- integrate sexuality into the rest of the personality

Regain intellectual competence through reading and engaging in other intellectually stimulating activities.

Address pre-cult conflicts such as family problems, academic anxiety, career-related confusion, disillusionment with society, and the like.

Address religious and philosophical issues, thus finding outlets for personal expression and commitment.

Set priorities and goals regarding: career, education, recreation, and the like (both long-term and short-term).

Work towards self-sufficiency:
- financial independence
  - learn (or relearn) budgeting skills,
  - establish and maintain a checking and savings account,
  - consider and implement the steps to secure a full-time, satisfying job, for example, pursue educational or licensing credentials, learn appropriate skills, prepare a resume.

Note: Many ex-cultists cringe at the notion of preparing a resumé, thinking, "How can those years in the cult be explained, concealed, or erased? What will an employer think if he finds out I was in a cult? Should I be truthful? I don't want to lie, but I may be forced to if I want to get a job.

The answer to these practical and ethical concerns varies, depending on the particular activities a cultist engaged in while in the cult. Those members who held outside jobs can simply list them and omit any mention of cult activities. However, those who were not employed may have to translate their volunteer cult activities into job-market language. If pressed, ex-cultists may feel obliged to explain their cult affiliation, and doing this is not the end of the world. In fact, some employers view the cult background as an interesting aspect of the ex-member's past. In general, though, we advise against mentioning the cult, as the experience tends to be misinterpreted by most persons. Finally, it may help to get suggestions from other ex-members who have already overcome this obstacle.

- emotional independence: strive for self-motivation, inner-directedness; ability to be alone and solve problems/conflicts alone; learn when and how to seek emotional support.
- acquire skills for managing a household, and prepare to (eventually) move out of parents' home.

Integrate the cult experience into the rest of one's life as an accepted, but not dominating, aspect of the past.

Tasks Facing Parents
- Taking care of yourself
- Learning to trust your child
- Allowing your child to make mistakes
- Helping your child define the tasks of reentry
- Helping your child define strategies for accomplishing these tasks
- Acknowledging and sympathizing with the disappointments
- Sharing in the joys
- Directing your child towards outside resources
- Pursuing other interests and commitments in addition to helping your child
- Integrating your child's cult experience as an accepted, but not dominating, part of your past.

Post-Cult: Noon

By Joan Carol Ross

The mirror has grown better-natured
I enter and endure
the storms and the doldrums,

the harsh and the soft,
the marshes and mountains
that taunt and confront,
challenge, comfort, caress.
Yes I flinch
I puzzle
I rant
But mostly the wind sings
the cloud weeps
and I respond.

APPENDIX A

Resource Organizations

Cult education and information organizations exist in most Western countries. Among the major organizations are the:

American Family Foundation (P.O. Box 336, Weston, MA 02193; 617-893-0930). Publisher of *Cults: What Parents Should Know*, AFF is a nonprofit, tax-exempt, research and educational organization founded in 1979. Staffed by professionals and guided by a distinguished advisory board, AFF collects information on cults and manipulative techniqes of persuasion and control, analyzes the information in order to advance understanding of the problem and possible solutions to it, and shares this understanding with professionals, the general public, and those needing help with cult involvements. AFF's extensive publications list can be found in Appendix B. AFF maintains lists of cult aware mental health professionals and lawyers. If you are interested in obtaining more information from AFF, please write or call to leave your name and address, and you will receive introductory information.

Cult Awareness Network (2421 W. Pratt Boulevard, Suite 1173, Chicago, IL 60645; 312-267-7777). The Cult Awareness Network (CAN) is a national, tax-exempt nonprofit educational organization, dedicated to promoting public awareness of the harmful effects of mind control. CAN confines its concerns to unethical or illegal practices and does not judge doctrine or belief. CAN consists of volunteers in more than 50 affiliates throughout the United States and Canada, and the organization FOCUS, a support group for former cult members.

Task Force on Missionaries and Cults (and Cult Hotline/Crisis Clinic), Jewish Community Relations Council of New York, 711 Third Ave., 13th Fl., New York, NY 10017, (212) 983-4800 (Task Force), (212) 860-8533 (Hotline/Crisis Clinic).

Commission on Missionaries and Cults (and Cult Clinic), Jewish Federation Council of Greater Los Angeles, 6505 Wilshire Blvd., Suite 802, Los Angeles, CA 90048, (213) 852-1234 (Task Force), (213) 852-1234, Ext. 2662 (Clinic)

Spiritual Counterfeits Project, Box 4308, Berkeley, CA 94704, (415) 524-9534

Committee on Cults and Missionaries, Greater Miami Jewish Federation, 4200 Biscayne Blvd., Miami, FL 33137, (305) 576-4000)

Cult Project/ Project Culte, 3460 Stanley St., Montreal, Quebec H3A 1R8, (514) 845-9171

Council on Mind Abuse (COMA), Box 575, Station Z, Toronto, Canada M5N 2Z6, (416) 484-1112

Overseas

Family Action, Information, and Rescue (F.A.I.R.), BCM Box 3535, Box 12, London, WCIN 3XX, U.K. Tel. (44) 1-1539-3940

Irish Family Foundation, Box 1628, Balls Bridge, Dublin 4, Ireland

Association Pour La Defense de La Famille et L'individu (ADFI), 4 Rue Flechier, 75009 Paris, France. Tel. (33) 1-42-85-15-52

Pastor Friedrich-W. Haack, Bavarian Lutheran Church. Bunzlauer Str. 28, D-8000 Munchen 50, West Germany. Tel. (49) 89-141-2841

Pro Juventud, Aribau, 226 INT. BJS., 08006 Barcelona, Spain. Tel. (34) 3-201-4886

Dialog Center International, Katrinebjergve 46, DK-8200 Aarhus N, Denmark. Tel. (45) 6-10-54-11

Concerned Parents, A.C., Box 1806, Haifa, Israel. Tel. (972) 4-71-85-22

Association Exposing Pseudo-Religious Cults, Box 900G, Melbourne, Australia 3001

The Jewish Center, Box 34, Balaclava, Victoria 3183, Australia Tel. (61) 3-527-5069

CCG Ministries, Box 6, No. Perth, West Australia. Tel. (61) 63- 444-6183